Vowel Sounds

Symbol	Examples
a	**a**ct, b**a**t
ā	d**ay**, **a**ge
âr	**air**, d**are**
ä	f**a**ther, st**a**r
e	**e**dge, t**e**n
ē	sp**ee**d, mon**ey**
ə*	**a**go, syst**e**m, easi**l**y, c**o**mpete, foc**u**s
ēr	d**ear**, p**ier**
i	f**i**t, **i**s
ī	sk**y**, b**i**te
o	n**o**t, w**a**sp
ō	n**o**se, **o**ver
ô	l**a**w, **o**rder
oi	n**oi**se, enj**oy**
o͞o	tr**ue**, b**oo**t
oo	p**u**t, l**oo**k
yo͞o	c**u**te, **u**nited
ou	l**ou**d, c**ow**
u	f**u**n, **u**p
ûr	l**ear**n, **ur**ge, butt**er**, w**or**d

*This symbol, the *schwa*, represents the sound of unaccented vowels. It sounds like "uh."

Symbol	Examples
ch	**ch**eap, ma**tch**, pi**c**ture
d	**d**oor, hea**d**
f	**f**an, lea**f**, **ph**one
g	**g**ive, do**g**
h	**h**er, be**h**ave
j	**j**ust, pa**g**e
k	**k**ing, ba**k**e, **c**ar
l	**l**eaf, ro**ll**
m	**m**y, ho**m**e
n	**n**ote, rai**n**
ng	si**ng**, ba**n**k
p	**p**ut, sto**p**
r	**r**ed, fa**r**
s	**s**ay, pa**ss**
sh	**sh**ip, pu**sh**
t	**t**o, le**t**
th	**th**in, wi**th**
TH	**TH**at, ba**TH**e
v	**v**alue, li**v**e
w	**w**ant, a**w**ay
y	**y**es, on**i**on
z	**z**oo, ma**z**e, ri**s**e
zh	plea**s**ure, vi**s**ion

Emily Marie Granadeño

Interactive Vocabulary
General Words

Roberta A. Bemis
Imperial Valley College

Patti C. Biley
Imperial Valley College

Amy E. Olsen
Imperial Valley College

New York San Francisco Boston
London Toronto Sydney Tokyo Singapore Madrid
Mexico City Munich Paris Capetown Hong Kong Montreal

Acquisitions Editor: Steven Rigolosi
Marketing Manager: Melanie Goulet
Supplements Editor: Donna Campion
Production Manager: Donna DeBenedictis
Project Coordination, Text Design, and Electronic Page Makeup: Elm Street Publishing Services, Inc.
Cover Designer/Manager: Nancy Danahy
Cover Photos: PhotoDisc, Inc.; Corbis (bottom right)
Art Studio: Burmar
Photo credits: p. 54, Corbis; p. 57, Archive Photos; p. 70, Jose Dupont/Jacana/Photo Researchers, Inc.
Photo Researcher: Karen Pugliano
Senior Manufacturing Manager: Dennis J. Para
Printer and Binder: Quebecor World/Dubuque
Cover Printer: Coral Graphic Services, Inc.

Copyright © 2001 by Addison Wesley Longman, Inc.

All rights reserved. No part of this publication may be reproduced, stored in a retrieval system, or transmitted, in any form or by any means, electronic, mechanical, photocopying, recording, or otherwise, without the prior written permission of the publisher. Printed in the United States.

Please visit our website at http://www.awlonline.com

ISBN 0-321-05496-2

12345678910-ARD-03020100

Dedications

To the students at Imperial Valley College.
—*Roberta Bemis*

To my family and church family for their encouragement.
—*Patti Biley*

To my friends and family for listening.
—*Amy Olsen*

Contents

Preface xi

▶ ▶ ▶ **Getting Started** 2

1 Cafeteria Views 8

2 Sports 12

3 School 16

4 Music 20

5 Communication 24

6 Word Parts I 28

7 Romance 32

8 Art 36

9 Time Management 40

10 Review: Focus on Chapters 1–9 44

p. 20

p. 12

p. 30

p. 36

11 Personalities 50

12 History 54

13 Politics 58

14 Friendship 62

15 Travel 66

p. 44

16 Pets 70

17 The Environment 74

18 Word Parts II 78

19 Volunteering 82

20 Complaints 86

p. 70

21 Review: Focus on Chapters 11–20 90

22 Television 96

23 Books 100

24 Movies 104

25 The Workplace 108

p. 104

26 **Computers** 112

27 **Personal Finance** 116

28 **Aviation** 120

29 **Languages** 124

30 **Review: Focus on Chapters 22–29** 128

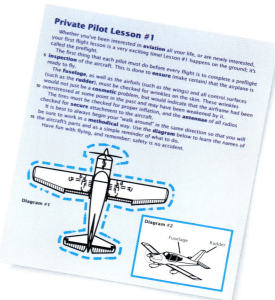
p. 120

Analogies Appendix   135
Limited Answer Key   137
Flash Cards   141
Inside Front Cover   Pronunciation Key
Inside Back Cover   Word List

Preface

Because students benefit greatly from increased word power, the study of vocabulary should be enjoyable. Unfortunately, vocabulary workbooks often lose sight of this goal. To help make the study of vocabulary an exciting and enjoyable part of college study, we have written *Interactive Vocabulary*.

The goal of this book—the first in a three-book series—is to make the study of vocabulary fun through a variety of thematic readings, interactive exercises, and self-tests. As a casual glimpse through the book will indicate, these activities involve writing, personal experience, art, and many other formats. The goal of these activities is simple: to utilize individual learning styles to help students learn new words in a large number of contexts.

Underlying the text's strong visual appeal is a strong underlying philosophy: an essential part of learning vocabulary is repeated exposure to a word. *Interactive Vocabulary* provides nine exposures to each word.

CONTENT OVERVIEW

Interactive Vocabulary is an ideal text for both classroom work and self-study. Each four-page chapter includes the following:

- **Thematic Reading:** Because most vocabulary is acquired through reading, each chapter begins with a thematic reading that introduces ten vocabulary words in context. These readings come in a variety of formats, from newspaper articles to comic strips to fliers. The goal is to show that new words may be encountered anywhere, not just in college textbooks. Rather than simply presenting a word list with definitions, we give students the opportunity to discover the meanings of these new words via context clues.

    The themes included in *Interactive Vocabulary* were chosen from areas most interesting to students of all ages. In choosing the words, we've been guided by four factors: (1) relation to the chapter theme, (2) use in popular magazines such as *Newsweek,* (3) listings in such frequency guides as *The American Heritage Word Frequency Book* and *The Educator's Word Frequency Guide,* and (4) our own experience in the developmental reading classroom.

- **Predicting:** The second page of each chapter contains a Predicting activity that gives students the chance to figure out the meaning of each vocabulary word before looking at the definition. The Predicting section helps students learn the value of context clues in determining the meaning of a word. (While the text does offer a full chapter on dictionary use, we strongly advocate the use of context clues as one of the most active methods of vocabulary development.)

- **Word List:** Following the Predicting activity is a list of the words with a pronunciation guide, the part of speech, and a brief definition. We wrote these definitions with the idea of keeping them simple and nontechnical. Some vocabulary texts provide complicated dictionary definitions that include words that students do not know; we've tried to make our definitions as friendly and as useful as possible.

- **Interactive Exercise:** Following the Word List is an Interactive Exercise that asks the reader to begin interacting actively with the vocabulary words. The activity may include writing, answering questions, or interviewing another person. The Interactive Exercises

give students the chance to really think about the meanings of the words, but more importantly, they encourage students to begin using the words actively.
- **Self-Tests:** Following the Interactive Exercise are Self-Tests in various formats. With these tests, students can monitor their comprehension. The tests include text and sentence completion, true/false situations, choosing synonyms, matching, and analogies. Some tests employ context-clue strategies such as synonyms, antonyms, and general meaning. Critical thinking skills are an important part of each test. (Answers to selected tests appear at the back of the book. Answers for all remaining exercises and tests appear in the Instructor's Manual.)

ADDITIONAL FEATURES

In addition to the thematic vocabulary chapters, *Interactive Vocabulary* includes a Getting Started chapter, two Word Parts chapters, three Review chapters, flash cards, and hint boxes. A pronunciation key appears on the inside front cover, and an alphabetical list of all vocabulary words (with page references) is included on the inside back cover.

- **Getting Started:** *Interactive Vocabulary* begins with an introductory chapter to familiarize students with some of the tools of vocabulary. The Parts of Speech section gives sample words and sentences for the eight parts of speech. Using the Dictionary dissects a sample dictionary entry and provides exercises on buying a dictionary and using guide words.
- **Word Parts Chapters:** The two Word Parts chapters introduce prefixes, roots, and suffixes used throughout this book. Students learn the meanings of these forms and sample words that illustrate the forms. Five self-tests in each chapter give students the opportunity to practice using the word parts.
- **Review Chapters:** Three Review chapters focus on the preceding eight or nine chapters. They divide the words into different activity groups and test students' cumulative knowledge. The words appear in artistic, dramatic, written, test, and puzzle formats. These repeated and varied exposures increase the likelihood that the words will be remembered not for one chapter or a test but for life.
- **Flash Cards:** At the back of the book is a series of flash cards with each chapter's vocabulary words, their pronunciations on the front and definitions on the back. Students can use these cards for self-study. Alternatively, instructors can use them for the supplemental activities and games that are outlined in the Instructor's Manual.
- **Hints:** Some chapters include hints for developing vocabulary skills. The hints are brief and practical, and students will be able to make use of them in all of their college courses.
- **Pronunciation Key:** On the inside front cover is a pronunciation key to help students understand the pronunciation symbols used in this text. The inside front cover also offers some additional guidelines on pronunciation issues.

THE TEACHING AND LEARNING PACKAGE

Each component of the teaching and learning package for *Interactive Vocabulary* has been carefully crafted to maximize the main text's value.

- **Instructor's Manual with Test Bank:** The Instructor's Manual, which is almost as long as the main text, includes options for additional classroom activities such as collaborative exercises and games. The Collaborative Exercises usually ask students to share their work on the Interactive Exercises in small groups or with the whole class. These exercises give students the opportunity to practice using the words with other people. Some of the Games can be copied and handed out as additional activities (such as crossword puzzles); others are suggestions for full-class activities (such as charades). Some games have winners, and some are just for fun. The games may involve acting, drawing, or writing.

Also included in the Instructor's Manual is a test-bank section, formatted for easy copying. The test bank includes Mastery Tests to accompany the review chapters as well as several full-book Mastery Tests, which can be used as final exams. ISBN: 0-321-05497-0.

- *Interactive Vocabulary* **CD-ROM:** In the computer age many students enjoy learning via computers. Available with this text is the *Interactive Vocabulary* CD-ROM, featuring additional exercises and tests that allow for even more interaction between the student and the words. The CD-ROM has an audio component that allows students to hear each chapter's thematic reading and the pronunciation of each word as often as they choose. Students are often reluctant to use the new words they learn because they aren't sure how to pronounce them. The pronunciation guides in each chapter do help to address this fear, but actually hearing the words spoken will give students greater confidence to use the words. Contact your AWL sales representative to order the student text packaged with the free CD-ROM.

FOR ADDITIONAL READING AND REFERENCE

- **The Dictionary Deal:** Two dictionaries can be shrink-wrapped with *Interactive Vocabulary* at a nominal fee. *The New American Webster Handy College Dictionary* is a paperback reference text with more than 100,000 entries. *Merriam Webster's Collegiate Dictionary,* Tenth Edition, is a hardback reference with a citation file of more than 14.5 million examples of English words drawn from actual usage. To take advantage of this special dictionary deal, contact your AWL sales representative.
- **The Longman Textbook Reader:** This free supplement, available with *Interactive Vocabulary,* offers five complete chapters from Addison Wesley Longman textbooks in the subjects of computer science, biology, psychology, communications, and business. Each chapter includes additional comprehension quizzes, critical-thinking questions, and group activities. For more details, consult your Addison Wesley Longman sales consultant.
- *Newsweek* **Alliance:** Instructors may choose to shrink-wrap a twelve-week subscription to *Newsweek* with any Longman text. The price of the subscription is 57¢ per issue (a total of $6.84 for the subscription). Available with the subscription is a free copy of *Interactive Guide to Newsweek*—a workbook for students who are using this text. In addition, *Newsweek* provides a wide variety of instructor supplements free to teachers, including maps, Skills Builders, and weekly quizzes. For more information on the *Newsweek* deal, please contact your AWL sales representative.

ACKNOWLEDGMENTS

We would like to thank the following reviewers for their helpful suggestions while the book took shape:

Kathy Beggs, Pikes Peak Community College
Diana Bosco, Suffolk County Community College
Janet Curtis, Fullerton College
Carol Dietrick, Miami-Dade Community College

Miriam Kinard, Trident Technical College

Belinda Klau, Imperial Valley College

John M. Kopec, Boston University

Maggi Miller, Austin Community College

Kerry Segel, Saginaw Valley State University

Susan Sandmeier, Columbia Basin College

Kathleen Sneddon, University of Nebraska, Lincoln

Shirley Wachtel, Middlesex Community College

Carolyn Wilkie, Indiana University of Pennsylvania

A special thank you goes to Steven Rigolosi, Acquisitions Editor, Basic Skills, at Addison Wesley Longman. Steve helped immensely with his enthusiasm and patience through the joys and challenges of creating a book that combines traditional and innovative approaches to vocabulary study. We would also like to express appreciation to the English Division at Imperial Valley College for its support and to Frances Beope of Counseling at IVC, who first suggested writing a book for our students.

We are proud to present a book that makes learning vocabulary fun.

Roberta A. Bemis
Patti C. Biley
Amy E. Olsen

Coming Soon

Book 2 of the Interactive Vocabulary Series:
  Active Vocabulary: General and Academic Words by Patti C. Biley and Amy E. Olsen

Book 3 of the Interactive Vocabulary Series:
  Academic Vocabulary: Academic Words by Roberta A. Bemis

Interactive Vocabulary
General Words

Getting Started

PARTS OF SPEECH

There are eight parts of speech. A word's part of speech is based on how it is used in a sentence. Words can, therefore, be more than one part of speech. For an example, note how *punch* is used below.

nouns: (n.) name a person, place, or thing
EXAMPLES: Ms. Lopez, New Orleans, lamp, warmth
Ms. Lopez enjoyed her *trip* to *New Orleans* where she bought a beautiful *lamp*. The *warmth* of the *sun* filled *Claire* with *happiness*. I drank five *cups* of the orange *punch*.

pronouns: (pron.) are used in place of a noun
EXAMPLES: I, me, you, she, he, it, her, we, they, my, which, that, anybody, everybody
Everybody liked the music at the party. *It* was the kind that made people want to dance. *They* bought a new car, *which* hurt their bank account.

verbs: (v.) express an action or state of being
EXAMPLES: enjoy, run, think, read, dance, am, is, are, was, were
Lily *read* an interesting book yesterday. I *am* tired. He *is* an excellent student. She *punched* the bully.

adjectives: (adj.) are used to modify (describe or explain) a noun or pronoun
EXAMPLES: pretty, old, two, expensive, red, small
The *old* car was covered with *red* paint on *one* side. The *two* women met for lunch at an *expensive* restaurant. The *punch* bowl was empty soon after Uncle Al got to the party.

adverbs: (adv.) are used to modify a verb, an adjective, or another adverb
EXAMPLES: very, shortly, first, too, soon, quickly, finally, furthermore, however
We will meet *shortly* after one o'clock. The *very* pretty dress sold *quickly*. I liked her; *however*, there was something strange about her.

prepositions: (prep.) are placed before a noun or pronoun to make a phrase that relates to other parts of the sentence
EXAMPLES: after, around, at, before, by, from, in, into, of, off, on, through, to, up, with
He told me to be *at* his house *around* noon. You must go *through* all the steps to do the job.

conjunctions: (conj.) are used to join words or other sentence elements and show a relationship between the connected items
EXAMPLES: and, but, or, nor, for, so, yet, after, although, because, if, since, than, when
I went to the movies, *and* I went to dinner on Tuesday. I will not go to the party this weekend *because* I have to study. I don't want to hear your reasons *or* excuses.

interjections: (interj.) are used to show surprise or emotion

EXAMPLES: oh, hey, wow, ah, ouch

Oh, I forgot to do my homework! *Wow,* I got an A on the test!

USING THE DICTIONARY

Do you think that using a dictionary is a sign of weakness? In reality, the opposite is true. Using a dictionary is a sign of a curious, growing, and flexible mind. If you develop the habit of using the dictionary when you're not quite sure about a word, you'll be sharing that habit with many of the finest minds on the planet.

Dictionary **entries** (the words and definitions) are arranged in alphabetical order. To help you find your word more quickly, the first and last entry words that appear on a page are listed at the top of that page. These are called **guide words**, because they help guide you to the word you are looking for. If the word you're looking for fits alphabetically between the two guide words, then you know that it's on that page.

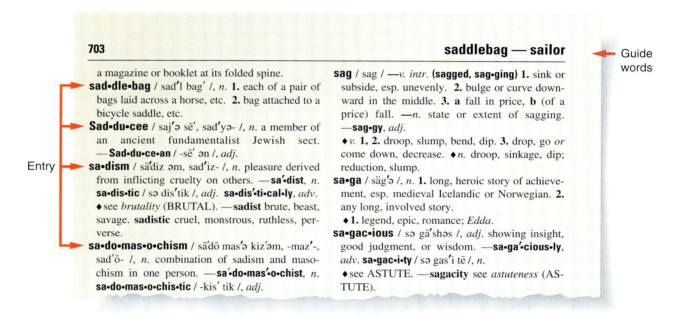

Source: *The Oxford Desk Dictionary and Thesaurus* (New York: Oxford University Press, 1997, p. 703.

Most dictionaries include the following information for each word:
- The **pronunciation**—the way a word sounds when it's spoken (including how it's broken into syllables and which syllable has the strongest accent). You can find an example of a pronunciation key on page 9 of this book. This key shows the symbols used to make the sounds of the words. Each dictionary has its own system for helping you to sound out the word. The key is usually in the front of the book, and occasionally a partial key may be found at the bottom of each page.
- The **part of speech** (noun, verb, adjective, adverb, etc.)
- The **definition** (the most common meaning is listed first, with less common meanings listed afterwards)

- An **example** of how the word is used in a sentence (often in *italics* and following each separate meaning)
- **Synonyms** and **antonyms** (a reference book called a **thesaurus** specializes in listing synonyms and antonyms)
- What language the word came from
- How to spell the different forms of the word (the different tenses of a verb, the adjective form, and so on)

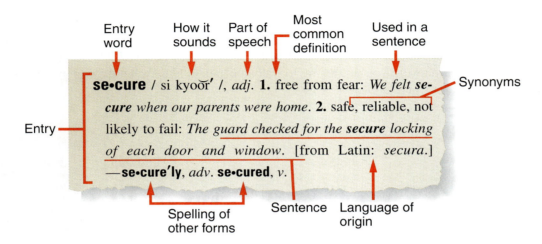

Although most dictionaries include the same information, some use simpler sentences to explain the words, some include illustrations, and some are easier to read. If you don't have a dictionary, or you don't like the one you have, try looking at several different dictionaries. Compare the different dictionaries to see if there is one that includes the features that help you the most. Look up the same word in several different dictionaries to see which explanation makes the most sense to you. Dictionaries are like cars; not all makes and models appeal to all people, but there is one that you'll like more than the others.

Here are a few dictionaries to consider when shopping for a general dictionary: *Webster's New World Dictionary, Oxford American Dictionary, Funk & Wagnalls Standard Dictionary,* and *Webster's Collegiate Dictionary.* Collegiate dictionaries make good general dictionaries for college students because they include words that you can expect to find in college reading material. Like most books today, dictionaries come in hardback, soft cover, and large print editions.

There are also special-use dictionaries that deal with words for certain topics, such as medical dictionaries, law dictionaries, and architectural dictionaries. These dictionaries specialize in words that would not be found in a good general dictionary, or that have a different meaning when used in the context of a specific subject. Also available are bilingual dictionaries (Spanish/English, French/English, Japanese/English, and so on).

Often, you will find a special section in the back of textbooks and technical books that looks like a dictionary. This feature is called a **glossary,** and it lists only words found in that book. The entry for each word may have many of the features of a general dictionary.

Before you look up a word in the dictionary, you should try to guess its meaning, and then look it up to see if you were correct. If you don't make the guess first, the next time you see the word the only thing you'll remember about it is that you've looked it up before!

Interactive Exercise

Rate the importance to you of each of the dictionary features listed below. Use #1 for the most important feature, #2 for the next most important, etc. (The rating is based on your preference, so there is no one right answer.)

_____ easy-to-understand pronunciation key

_____ a pronunciation key on each page

_____ lots of definitions for each word

_____ sentences for each definition showing how the word is used

_____ synonyms for each word

_____ antonyms for each word

_____ illustrations

_____ large number of entries

_____ spellings for the different forms (adv., v., n.)

_____ what language the word came from

Which Dictionary Should I Buy?

Match the type of dictionary to the statements below.

a. thesaurus
b. special use: English/Russian
c. hardcover
d. paperback
e. collegiate
f. special use: medical
g. large print

_____ 1. I need a gift for a medical student.

_____ 2. I have difficulty reading small print.

_____ 3. I want to buy a dictionary that is both inexpensive and easy to carry.

_____ 4. I'm studying Russian.

_____ 5. I don't care how much it costs; I want the book to last a long time.

_____ 6. I want lots of synonyms and antonyms.

_____ 7. This is my first year at the university.

Using Guide Words

Use the sample guide words to figure out on which page the entry word will be found. Write the page number next to the entry word. There may be more than one entry word on a page.

Page	Guide Words
35	aquarium/arch
36	archeology/argon
37	argot/arm
503	mincemeat/mineral
504	mineralogy/mink
505	minnow/mire
525	narcotic/nativity
526	natural/navy

_____ 1. miner

_____ 2. arid

_____ 3. minus

_____ 4. archer

_____ 5. narrow

_____ 6. argument

_____ 7. nautical

_____ 8. minimum

_____ 9. arable

_____ 10. ministry

HINT

It is possible to understand the meaning of a word without knowing how to pronounce it correctly. BUT sometimes when you sound out a new word (using phonics) you realize you've heard it before, and that may help you to understand the meaning.

6   GETTING STARTED

Crossword Puzzle

Use the following words to complete the crossword puzzle. You will use each word once.

Vocabulary Words

- antonyms
- definition
- entry
- glossary
- guide
- large
- paper
- pronunciation
- special
- speech
- synonyms

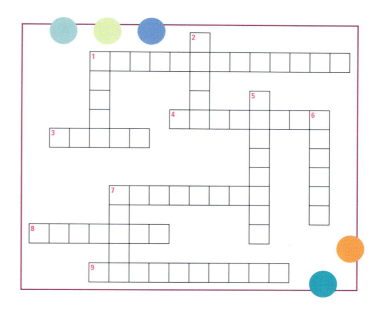

Across
1. the type of key that shows how to say a word
3. the type of print that is easiest to read
4. words that mean the same
7. a mini-dictionary in the back of a textbook
8. examples of this type of dictionary: bilingual, medical, law
9. the meaning

Down
1. the type of book cover that is soft (these also cost the least)
2. the name for the listed word plus the information given for it
5. words that have the opposite meaning
6. Nouns, verbs, prepositions, adverbs, adjectives are all called parts of _____.
7. the words at the top of the page that show if your word is on the page

© 2001 Addison Wesley Longman, Inc.

GETTING STARTED

CHAPTER 1

Cafeteria Views

Predicting

Circle the definition that seems to best fit each vocabulary word. If you have difficulty, return to the reading on page 8, and underline any context clues you find. These clues can help you guess the word's meaning. When you have made your predictions, check your answers against the Word List below. Use the boxes to checkmark those words whose definitions you missed—these are the words you'll want to study closely.

NOTE: You may want to cover the Word List below with a piece of paper so you don't accidentally see the definitions as you do the Predicting exercise.

☐ 1. **antonym** (bubble 2)
   a. home of ants
   b. word that means the same
   c. word that means the opposite

☐ 2. **predict** (bubble 4)
   a. to worry
   b. to tell in advance
   c. to get money in advance

☐ 3. **synonym** (bubble 6)
   a. a place of worship
   b. word with a similar meaning
   c. word that means the opposite

☐ 4. **thematic** (bubble 9)
   a. pertaining to a topic
   b. a type of disease
   c. something used in healing

☐ 5. **analogy** (bubble 10)
   a. a comparison
   b. a type of ghost
   c. a way of speaking

☐ 6. **interactive** (bubble 12)
   a. revolving inside the solar system
   b. moving something around in the room
   c. requiring active thought and communication

☐ 7. **context clues** (bubble 14)
   a. a mystery
   b. words around another word that give hints about its meaning
   c. a game where the winner gets a prize

☐ 8. **phonics** (bubble 16)
   a. using the telephone
   b. playing the telephone game
   c. sounding out a word

☐ 9. **collaborative** (bubble 17)
   a. collecting money at church
   b. eating with others
   c. working together

☐ 10. **diligent** (bubble 18)
   a. working in a careful way
   b. working in a careless way
   c. working during summer

Word List

analogy [ə nal′ ə jē]	n.	a comparison; likeness
antonym [an′ tə nim]	n.	word that means the opposite
collaborative [kə lab′ ûr ə tiv′]	adj.	working together
context clues [kon′ tekst klōōz′]	n.	words around another word that give hints about its meaning
diligent [dil′ ə jənt]	adj.	steady and energetic; careful
interactive [in′ tûr ak′ tiv]	adj.	requiring active thought and communication; making connections
phonics [fon′ iks]	n.	a reading method in which letters are associated with their sounds
predict [pri dikt′]	v.	to tell in advance
synonym [sin′ ə nim]	n.	word with a similar meaning
thematic [thē mat′ ik]	adj.	pertaining to a subject or topic

Interactive Exercise

Write a note to a classmate about your attitude toward studying vocabulary words. Use at least five of the vocabulary words introduced in this chapter. Use the space below to draft your note.

Dear _____ ,

_____
_____
_____
_____
_____
_____
_____
_____
_____
_____
_____
_____
_____

                                                                                                                      _____

HINT
Flash Cards

You will find flash cards for the words in every lesson at the back of your textbook. Carefully tear them out and cut them apart as you begin a new lesson. You can carry them with a rubber band or on a key chain after you punch a hole in the top left corner of each card. Make a habit of carrying these cards with you. Then, when you have some free time—even five minutes—you can quiz yourself.

    Look at the word, and try to memorize its meaning. Try to remember sentences from the chapter that use the word. Say them to yourself. You may need to look back at the chapter at first, but with time and repetition, you will remember them. Then, work on making up sentences of your own. These activities can be especially helpful if you work with a partner—a classmate or another person. One partner shows a card, and the other pronounces the word and gives its definition.

Self-Tests

1 Match each term with its synonym for Set One and with its antonym for Set Two.

SET ONE SYNONYMS

_____ 1. diligent   a. words around another word
_____ 2. phonics   b. comparison
_____ 3. analogy   c. steady
_____ 4. collaborative   d. associating sounds with words
_____ 5. context clues   e. together

SET TWO ANTONYMS

_____ 6. thematic   f. antonym
_____ 7. predict   g. isolated
_____ 8. interactive   h. synonym
_____ 9. antonym   i. discuss the past
_____ 10. synonym   j. unfocused

2 Pick the best word from below to complete the sentence. Use each word once.

1. I went to see a fortune-teller to hear her _____ whether I would be rich someday.

2. The _____ topic for our first paper in English class was technology.

3. I listened to ten _____ tapes in the reading lab to improve my pronunciation.

4. The student made an interesting _____ between writing a paper and riding a bike.

5. The woman wanted to become an executive in the company, so she was _____ at her job.

6. Making a movie is a _____ project because it involves writers, actors, technicians, and the director to put it together.

7. When I am reading and come across a word I don't know, I look for _____ to help me figure out the meaning.

8. Using a computer can be _____ because some programs tell you if your answer is right or wrong, and then you can think about your choices and make changes.

9. When I want to stop repeating the same word in a paper, but I need another word with the same meaning, I look in a thesaurus to find a _____.

10. *Stubborn* and *flexible* are important _____ to learn. I discovered the difference when my friends told me I was going to have to stop being stubborn and be more flexible or they couldn't see me anymore.

Vocabulary Words

synonym
interactive
thematic
collaborative
antonyms
diligent
analogy
phonics
predict
context clues

CHAPTER 1 CAFETERIA VIEWS

CHAPTER 2

Sports

VOLLEYBALL TEAM **TRIUMPHS** AGAIN!

In another **stunning** victory, the women's volleyball team defeated Lincoln College with scores of 15 to 2 and 15 to 5 in the best two out of three last Friday in the gym. Lincoln is known as a tough team, but the scores obviously show that Central's team this year is ready for anyone.

The team's coach, Edna Schultz, said, "I know this is a very talented group of women. Some of them were inexperienced when we began, but through disciplined workouts they have become great players." She explained that the team's **regimen** can be **grueling** because the players practice six days a week for two to three hours at a time, and they do running and weight workouts. Out of the gym, they watch what they eat. They also put a lot of time into their studies. "The victory was not a **fluke**; we are a team who will keep winning," added Coach Schultz.

The coach's enthusiasm is matched by that of team members. Denise Watson noted, "When our team is **confronted** by tough **opposition**, we just try harder." According to Rosemary Cortes, "Any team that comes against us is going to find that we are not easily **flustered**. One reason we don't get upset is because of the **intense** workouts Ms. Schultz establishes for us. We are prepared to meet anyone."

It is attitudes like these that will keep the team on top all season. The next game will be Friday, October 13, in the Madison College gym at 7 P.M. Come out and support a **dedicated** group of players and a hardworking coach.

Predicting

Circle the definition that seems to best fit each vocabulary word. If you have difficulty, return to the reading on page 12, and underline any context clues you find. These clues can help you guess the word's meaning. When you have made your predictions, check your answers against the Word List below. Use the boxes to checkmark those words whose definitions you missed—these are the words you'll want to study closely.

NOTE: You may want to cover the Word List below with a piece of paper so you don't accidentally see the definitions as you do the Predicting exercise.

❏ 1. **triumph** (headline)
   a. to win
   b. to be defeated
   c. to skip

❏ 2. **stunning** (line 2)
   a. ordinary
   b. amazing
   c. fast

❏ 3. **regimen** (line 19)
   a. a king
   b. a practice area
   c. a plan

❏ 4. **grueling** (line 19)
   a. easy
   b. exhausting
   c. fighting

❏ 5. **fluke** (line 27)
   a. a lucky chance
   b. a musical instrument
   c. part of an elephant

❏ 6. **confront** (line 33)
   a. to face head on
   b. to move behind
   c. to step aside

❏ 7. **opposition** (line 34)
   a. a peasant
   b. a small animal
   c. a contestant you are playing against

❏ 8. **fluster** (line 38)
   a. to give
   b. to upset
   c. to calm

❏ 9. **intense** (line 39)
   a. sleep outdoors
   b. to an extreme degree
   c. automatic

❏ 10. **dedicated** (line 48)
   a. devoted
   b. pained
   c. careless

Word List

confront [kən frunt′]	v.	to face head on
dedicated [ded′ ə kā′ tid]	adj.	devoted to a cause
dedicate [ded′ ə kāt′]	v.	to give one's talents to; to devote
fluke [flo͞ok]	n.	a lucky chance
fluster [flus′ tûr]	n.	a state of confusion
	v.	to upset; to cause confused behavior
grueling [gro͞o′ ə ling]	adj.	tiring; exhausting
intense [in tens′]	adj.	to an extreme degree; deep
opposition [äp′ ə zish′ ən]	n.	a contestant you are matched against; disagreement
regimen [rej′ ə mən, -men′]	n.	a plan; discipline
stunning [stun′ ing]	adj.	impressive in excellence or beauty; amazing
triumph [trī′ əmpf]	v.	to win; to overcome
	n.	the joy of victory

Interactive Exercise

Answer the following questions as they apply to your life:

1. To what are you most dedicated? _____
2. What most flusters you? _____
3. What was the most grueling experience you've had? _____
   _____
4. What is the toughest opposition you've faced? _____
5. Where have you seen the most stunning view? _____
6. What is the toughest problem you have confronted? _____
7. What has been the biggest fluke in your life? _____
8. What is the most intense experience you've had? _____
   _____
9. What is the hardest regimen you've had to follow? _____
   _____
10. What is your greatest triumph? _____

Self-Tests

1 Put a T for true or F for false next to each sentence.

____ 1. When confronted with a problem, sleeping on it can be a good idea.

____ 2. Mother Theresa was dedicated to helping others.

____ 3. Winning the lottery is a fluke.

____ 4. Being prepared for a test flusters most people.

____ 5. Climbing Mount Everest would be grueling.

____ 6. Writing a book is an intense experience.

____ 7. A parent and teenager agreeing on the time to come home from a date shows opposition.

____ 8. Getting up when you want and eating anything you want shows a strict dietary regimen.

____ 9. Sunsets are usually stunning.

____ 10. Finding a cure for cancer would be a triumph.

Finish these headlines using the vocabulary words. Use each word once.

Vocabulary Words

| confronts | dedicates | fluke | flustered | grueling |
| intense | opposition | regimen | stunning | triumphs |

1. Huge Sports _____ : Against All Odds U.S. Wins the World Cup!

2. Tiger Woods Gets _____ ; Ends Up in the Sand Trap

3. Tour de France Update: Ten Riders Fade in _____ Mountain Stage

4. The _____ that Wins — Jordan's Training Secrets for Guaranteed Success

5. _____ Quadruple Axel Wows Judges

6. Wimbledon Veteran Faces Tough _____ from Newcomer

7. New Information on Steroid Use _____ the NFL

8. Pitcher _____ His Talents to Youth Camp

9. Gymnast _____ : From Spinal Injury to Gold Medal

10. _____ Wind Delays Slalom Events

CHAPTER 3

School

A New Student at the Community College

Claudia Marquez had lived in northern Mexico all her life. The day she left for the United States, her mother had cried. "My daughter, I'll miss you, but your brother will take good care of you in San Diego. Promise me that you'll study hard!" Claudia had promised.

Claudia's brother Alex had begun his studies at a community college and had later earned a university degree. Now he was a successful businessman. Soon after Claudia's arrival, Alex spoke to her about attending college. "**Registration** at City College starts in two weeks. You need to **apply** before the **deadline**. If you don't, it will be too late. But first you need to see a **counselor** to give you advice on your courses. Let's go tomorrow."

The next morning, Claudia explored the college **campus** with her brother. He pointed out the library, cafeteria, bookstore, gym, and the administration building before he left her at the counseling center. While Claudia waited, she started filling out an application and spoke to two friendly girls from Japan. Then her counselor, Mrs. Cortes, asked about her **career** plans. Did she want to study nursing? Computer science? Claudia was undecided about her **major**, but she was interested in math and business. The counselor said that the **faculty** in both areas were excellent.

Claudia went to take placement tests in English and mathematics at the campus **assessment** center. As a new student, she had to attend an **orientation** session to find out more about the college. She was happy to be starting her new life as a college student. She would keep her promise to her mother. She would study hard and be successful.

Predicting

Circle the definition that seems to best fit each vocabulary word. If you have difficulty, return to the reading on page 16, and underline any context clues you find. These clues can help you guess the word's meaning. When you have made your predictions, check your answers against the Word List below. Use the boxes to checkmark those words whose definitions you missed—these are the words you'll want to study closely.

NOTE: You may want to cover the Word List below with a piece of paper so you don't accidentally see the definitions as you do the Predicting exercise.

❑ 1. **registration** (line 8)
   a. information
   b. procedure
   c. official entry

❑ 2. **apply** (line 9)
   a. to fix
   b. to request formally
   c. to promise to pay

❑ 3. **deadline** (line 9)
   a. latest time to do something
   b. only chance
   c. halftime

❑ 4. **counselor** (line 10)
   a. gym teacher
   b. registrar
   c. advisor

❑ 5. **campus** (line 12)
   a. college center
   b. buildings and grounds of a school
   c. campsite

❑ 6. **career** (line 17)
   a. travel
   b. profession
   c. advice

❑ 7. **major** (line 18)
   a. plan of studies
   b. income
   c. career

❑ 8. **faculty** (line 19)
   a. building
   b. facilities
   c. teachers

❑ 9. **assessment** (line 22)
   a. testing
   b. acceptance
   c. assignment

❑ 10. **orientation** (line 23)
   a. technical training
   b. study skills
   c. program to help students adjust

Word List

apply [ə plī′] *v.* 1. to make a formal request 2. (apply oneself) to try hard

assessment [ə ses′ mənt] *n.* testing; evaluation

campus [kam′ pəs] *n.* buildings and grounds of a school, college, or university

career [kə rēr′] *n.* a profession or occupation

counselor [koun′ sə lûr] *n.* advisor; person who counsels

deadline [ded′ līn] *n.* latest possible time for something to be completed

faculty [fak′ əl tē] *n.* teachers of a school, college, or university

major [mā jûr] *n.* principal area of study

orientation [ôr′ ē ən tā′ shən] *n.* program intended to help people adapt

registration [rej′ ə strā′ shən] *n.* formal process of entering a class or program

Interactive Exercise

Draw a simple map of your school or college *campus.* Label the map with at least five vocabulary words, showing where you go to do activities at your school. For example, show where you go for *registration* and *orientation,* where *faculty* offices are located, and where students can visit their *counselors.*

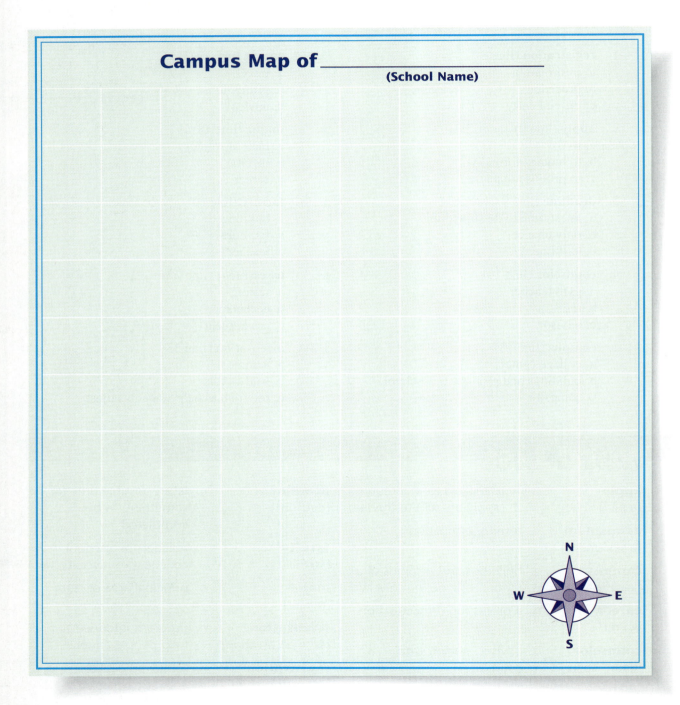

Campus Map of _____
(School Name)

Self-Tests

1 Write the letter of the vocabulary word next to the best definition.

1. ____ instructors
2. ____ latest time
3. ____ signing up for a class
4. ____ occupation, profession
5. ____ school grounds
6. ____ main area of study
7. ____ request admission
8. ____ person who gives advice
9. ____ program to help students adapt
10. ____ testing

a. campus
b. counselor
c. major
d. assessment
e. faculty
f. career
g. orientation
h. apply
i. registration
j. deadline

HINT

If you get stuck on one question, go to the next one. When you finish answering the ones that are easy for you, see which questions and words are left. With fewer choices the answers should be easier to find.

2 Fill in the blanks of Claudia's letter with the appropriate vocabulary word.

Dear Mom,

I'm writing this letter to you in English, so you'll know how much I've learned. If you don't understand it, you can look at the translation on the other side!

I've just completed my first semester of classes at the community college, and I'm taking classes in my _____, which is business. So much has happened since I arrived. Alex has helped me a lot. Back before school started in the fall, he took me to the college _____ and showed me around. Then I had to go talk to a _____. We talked about my plans for a future _____. I did a lot of other things that day, too. One important thing was that I had to _____ to the college for admission. It took a long time to fill out the form. I had to take some tests at the _____ center, too. A couple of days later I had to go back to the college for _____. They told us all the things we needed to know about being in college. Then there was _____ for classes. There were a lot of long lines there.

I only took English and Psychology in the fall, because it was my first semester. I didn't miss any classes and I made all the _____ for my assignments. I've kept my promise to you, Mama. I've really learned a lot and I got good grades! Write soon.

Love,
Claudia

Vocabulary Words
apply
assessment
campus
career
counselor
deadlines
faculty
major
orientation
registration

CHAPTER 3 SCHOOL 19

CHAPTER 4

Music

The Chorus Needs New Voices!!!!

Rehearsals to begin for the Spring Musical **Revue**

5 The practices will lead to an **enchanting** night of skits, songs, and dances in May

Come now and join the fun of sharing your singing abilities

Novices and **Experts** Welcome

10 We need all voices from the highs of the **soprano** to the lows of the **bass** section

If you are unsure of your musical **aptitude**, come to the tryouts and
15 we will happily give you **feedback**

See you Tuesday, October 6 from 3–6 in the auditorium

Predicting

Circle the definition that seems to best fit each vocabulary word. If you have difficulty, return to the reading on page 20, and underline any context clues you find. These clues can help you guess the word's meaning. When you have made your predictions, check your answers against the Word List below. Use the boxes to checkmark those words whose definitions you missed—these are the words you'll want to study closely.

NOTE: You may want to cover the Word List below with a piece of paper so you don't accidentally see the definitions as you do the Predicting exercise.

☐ 1. **chorus** (line 1)
   a. the basics
   b. a loud noise
   c. a group of people singing

☐ 2. **rehearsal** (line 4)
   a. a ballroom
   b. practice
   c. adventure

☐ 3. **revue** (line 4)
   a. a park
   b. a show
   c. a river

☐ 4. **enchanting** (line 5)
   a. depressing
   b. scary
   c. charming

☐ 5. **novice** (line 9)
   a. a beginner
   b. someone who is very good
   c. a painful experience

☐ 6. **expert** (line 9)
   a. new at something
   b. a person who loves cats
   c. a person with a special skill

☐ 7. **soprano** (line 11)
   a. low singing voice
   b. the lead singer
   c. the highest singing voice

☐ 8. **bass** (line 12)
   a. high singing voice
   b. the off-key singer
   c. the singer with the lowest range

☐ 9. **aptitude** (line 14)
   a. a talent
   b. a high place
   c. an injury

☐ 10. **feedback** (line 15)
   a. a response
   b. extreme hunger
   c. a part of the body

Word List

aptitude [ap′ tə tōō d′] *n.* 1. talent 2. quickness in learning; intelligence

bass [bās] *n.* the singer with the lowest pitch or range

chorus [kôr′ əs] *n.* 1. a group of people singing at the same time *v.* 2. to sing or speak at the same time

enchanting [en chan′ ting] *adj.* charming; captivating

expert [ek′ spûrt] *n.* a person who has a special skill or knowledge in a field
[ik spûrt′] *adj.* having a special skill from practice

feedback [fēd′ bak′] *n.* a reaction or response to a particular activity

novice [nov′ əs] *n.* a beginner

rehearsal [ri hûr′ səl] *n.* a practice, usually for a public performance

revue [ri vyōō ′] *n.* a show featuring skits, songs, and dances

soprano [sə pran′ ō, -prä′ nō] *n.* the highest singing voice found in some women and in young boys

Interactive Exercise

Pretend you went to the chorus tryouts, and write a journal/diary entry describing your experience. Use at least seven of the ten vocabulary words in the entry.

Dear Journal,

HINT

If you feel blocked when doing a writing exercise, try these prewriting techniques:

- **Freewriting:** Write without stopping for five minutes about your topic. Put down any ideas that come to mind.
- **Brainstorming:** Write your topic at the top of a piece of paper; then list any words or phrases under it that quickly come to you.
- **Clustering:** Circle your topic in the middle of a piece of paper. Make lines from it, and fill circles with ideas related to your topic. Again, jot down the ideas quickly.

CHAPTER 4   MUSIC

Self-Tests

1. Circle the word that correctly completes each sentence.

1. "This part is just for the high voices—(bass, soprano) section, get ready," yelled the conductor.

2. The practice was horrible. We postponed the (rehearsal, revue) until next week when people could come prepared to go over their lines.

3. I didn't have much (aptitude, feedback) for singing, so I put my skills where they were needed and designed the set.

4. The teacher didn't spend much time with the (novices, experts) because they had practiced the songs all last year.

5. We found the music (enchanting, chorus) due to its beautiful melody.

6. The (enchanting, chorus) was tired after rehearsing for six hours; they all went home to rest their voices.

7. The (novices, experts) had to practice a little longer because they had not sung the songs last year.

8. I really appreciated the conductor's (aptitude, feedback) about my singing.

9. We knew the (rehearsal, revue) would be the best ever because we had the funniest skits and the most graceful dancers.

10. I thought the (bass, soprano) voices, with their low range, sounded like the rumble of thunder in the distance.

2. Finish the story using the vocabulary words. Use each word once.

Vocabulary Words
- novice
- bass
- enchanting
- sopranos
- aptitude
- feedback
- revue
- rehearsals
- chorus
- expert

I love listening to music, but I can't sing. When my roommate, Katy, and I came home from the college's _____, we were both excited about the great dancing we'd seen. We also enjoyed the _____ songs. The _____ was so professional. I was especially impressed with the _____ section. I couldn't believe how low those guys' voices were. Katy liked the _____ better; she kept raving about the high notes they could sing. Katy loves to sing, and she wanted me to join her at the _____ for the spring musical she was practicing for. I told her I had no _____ for singing. She said that was just the _____ in me talking. She offered to listen to me and give me honest _____. I warned her it wouldn't be pretty. I began "Somewhere Over the Rainbow," and she stopped me fast. Katy's advice: "Stick to drawing; you're an _____ at that."

CHAPTER 5

Communication

Making Communication Easier

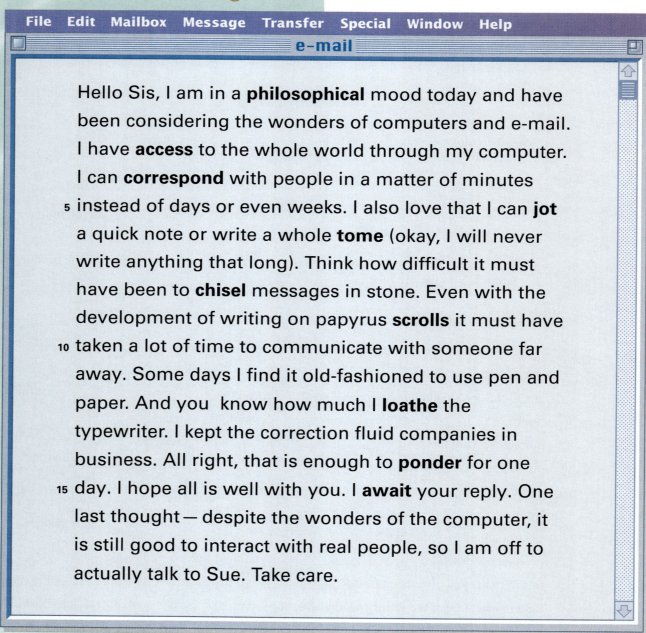

Hello Sis, I am in a **philosophical** mood today and have been considering the wonders of computers and e-mail. I have **access** to the whole world through my computer. I can **correspond** with people in a matter of minutes
5 instead of days or even weeks. I also love that I can **jot** a quick note or write a whole **tome** (okay, I will never write anything that long). Think how difficult it must have been to **chisel** messages in stone. Even with the development of writing on papyrus **scrolls** it must have
10 taken a lot of time to communicate with someone far away. Some days I find it old-fashioned to use pen and paper. And you know how much I **loathe** the typewriter. I kept the correction fluid companies in business. All right, that is enough to **ponder** for one
15 day. I hope all is well with you. I **await** your reply. One last thought — despite the wonders of the computer, it is still good to interact with real people, so I am off to actually talk to Sue. Take care.

Predicting

Circle the definition that seems to best fit each vocabulary word. If you have difficulty, return to the reading on page 24, and underline any context clues you find. These clues can help you guess the word's meaning. When you have made your predictions, check your answers against the Word List below. Use the boxes to checkmark those words whose definitions you missed—these are the words you'll want to study closely.

NOTE: You may want to cover the Word List below with a piece of paper so you don't accidentally see the definitions as you do the Predicting exercise.

❏ 1. **philosophical** (line 1)
   a. thoughtful
   b. wild
   c. disgusting

❏ 2. **access** (line 3)
   a. the ability to enter
   b. well done
   c. too much

❏ 3. **correspond** (line 4)
   a. to take a walk
   b. to drink
   c. to write someone

❏ 4. **jot** (line 5)
   a. to travel widely
   b. to write quickly
   c. to sleep late

❏ 5. **tome** (line 6)
   a. a big book
   b. a menu
   c. a place someone is buried

❏ 6. **chisel** (line 8)
   a. to dance
   b. to stir
   c. to carve

❏ 7. **scroll** (line 9)
   a. short trees
   b. a fight
   c. a roll of paper

❏ 8. **loathe** (line 12)
   a. to hate
   b. to love
   c. to want

❏ 9. **ponder** (line 14)
   a. to swim
   b. to fly
   c. to think

❏ 10. **await** (line 15)
   a. to lift weights
   b. to wait for
   c. to weigh oneself

Word List

access [ak′ ses] — *n.* state of being able to approach or enter; *v.* to get

await [ə wāt′] — *v.* 1. to wait for 2. to be in store for

chisel [chiz′ əl] — *v.* to cut or carve; *n.* a metal tool with a sharp edge used to cut stone, wood, or metal

correspond [kôr′ ə spond′] — *v.* 1. to communicate by letter, usually over a period of time 2. to be in agreement

jot [jot] — *v.* to write briefly and fast

loathe [lō TH] — *v.* to detest, hate

philosophical [fil′ ə sof′ i kəl] — *adj.* thoughtful; serene; wise

ponder [pon′ dər] — *v.* to consider carefully; reflect

scroll [skrōl] — *n.* a roll of paper with writing on it

tome [tōm] — *n.* any book, especially a large or scholarly book

Interactive Exercise

Answer the following questions:

1. What is something you loathe? Why? _____

2. What are three occasions when you might jot something down?
   _____   _____   _____

3. What book can you think of that qualifies as a tome? _____

4. What should all people have access to? _____

5. If you could correspond with one famous person, who would it be? Why?
   _____

6. What was the last decision you had to ponder? _____

7. What event do you eagerly await? _____

8. Where might you find a scroll? _____

9. What are you philosophical about? _____
   _____

10. If you were going to chisel a message, what material would you pick? Why?
    _____

HINT
Use It or Lose It

You may have heard this expression before, but it is as true with vocabulary as with many other things that you do. When you learn a new word in this class, you must take an important step before the word is really part of *your* vocabulary. This step is simple: Use it outside the classroom. When you feel that you understand the word and have practiced it in class, you must use it—not once but as much as you can. If you continue to use it—even if you don't feel comfortable doing this at first—the word will become part of your active vocabulary. *It will belong to you.*

If you make no effort to use the word, you will probably forget it when the class is over. Learning vocabulary is all about using the words, not about memorizing a definition. Think about this: If you know the definition of a word but can't use it when you are speaking or writing, what good is it to you?

Self-Tests

1. Write the vocabulary word on the line next to the situation it best fits. Use each word once.

Vocabulary Words

ponder	correspond	tome	loathe	philosophical
jot	access	await	chisel	scroll

1. about not winning an argument _____
2. a phone call from home _____
3. whether to change jobs _____
4. unroll the message from the king _____
5. with my pen pal _____
6. a message on marble _____
7. a grocery list _____
8. getting junk mail _____
9. having the client files at my fingertips _____
10. Tolstoy's novel *War and Peace* _____

2. In each group, circle the word that does not have a connection to the other three words.

Example: write   (ignore)   reply   correspond

When you correspond, you reply or write to a person. *Ignore* is not related to the other words.

1. reflect	ponder	think	do
2. tool	chisel	carve	paint
3. book	picture	dictionary	tome
4. jot	list	essay	note
5. detest	love	loathe	hate
6. scroll	message	roll	yelling
7. await	patience	rush	prepared
8. entry	access	blocked	approachable
9. depressed	calm	quiet	philosophical
10. same	correspond	different	agreement

CHAPTER 5   COMMUNICATION

CHAPTER 6

Word Parts I

Look for words with these **prefixes**, **roots**, and/or **suffixes** as you work through this book. You may have already seen some of them, and you will see others in later chapters. Learning basic word parts can help you figure out what unfamiliar words mean. (You will get more practice with word parts in chapter 18.)

prefix: a word part that is added to the beginning of a word and changes the meaning of the root
root: a word's basic part with its essential meaning
suffix: a word part that is added to the end of a word and signifies its part of speech

WORD PART	MEANING	EXAMPLES AND DEFINITIONS
Prefixes		
pre-	before	*predict:* to tell or say in advance
		preview: to see before
inter-	between	*interactive:* making connections between things
		international: between nations or countries
re-	again	*rehearsal:* a practice (to do something again)
		review: to look at something again
dis-	away from, not	*disorganized:* not organized
		disappear: move away from sight
con-, col-	together, with	*context:* a situation; involved with other elements
		collaborative: working together
Roots		
-dic-, -dict-	say, speak	*predict:* to tell or say in advance
		dictation: the process of saying or reading aloud to be recorded or written by someone else
-man-, -manu-	hand	*manuscript:* a handwritten document
		manually: done by hand
-phon-	sound	*phonics:* the study of sounds
		telephone: a device for hearing sound from far away
-chron-	time	*chronological:* following time order
		chronic: all the time
-pas-, -pat-, -path-	feeling, disease	*sympathy:* understanding someone's feelings
		psychopath: a person with a disease of the mind

WORD PART	MEANING	EXAMPLES AND DEFINITIONS
Suffixes		
-or, -er	one who	*counselor:* a person who counsels or gives advice *baker:* a person who bakes
-tion, -ation	condition, act of	*opposition:* the act of opposing or being in conflict *action:* condition of being active or doing
-ment	action, state of being	*assessment:* state of assessing or measuring *merriment:* the state of being merry
-ous, -ious, -ose	full of	*monotonous:* full of monotony; boring *cautious:* full of caution, careful
-ic, -al	relating to	*thematic:* relating to a theme or topic *musical:* relating to music

Self-Tests

1 Read the definition, and supply the appropriate word from the list below. Use each word once. The meaning of the word part is underlined to help you make the connection. Refer to the Words Parts list (page 28 and above) if you need help.

1. to say before _____

2. to tell again _____

3. to work together _____

4. to be able to handle _____

5. relating to time order _____

6. a person who is wise _____

7. the state of being charmed _____

8. to feel strongly about _____

9. condition of being false _____

10. full of courage _____

Vocabulary Words
enchantment
manage
passionate
predict
chronological
courageous
relate
philosopher
imitation
collaborate

2 Finish the sentences with the meaning of each word part from the list at the right. Use each meaning once. The word part is underlined to help you make the connection.

1. When you go to a preview of a movie, you see it _____ other people do.

2. The Olympics is an international event. This means it is held _____ different countries.

3. To have chronic pain means to have pain all the _____ or constantly.

4. An actor is a _____ acts.

5. If someone is feeling merriment, he or she is in the _____ merry.

6. If you have to repeat a class, you have to take it _____.

7. A psychopath is a person with a mental _____.

8. If you do something manually, you do it by _____.

9. If you dislike someone, you do _____ like him or her.

10. Something comical is _____ comedy.

not
hand
person who
disease
before
related to
between
state of being
again
time

 3 Finish the story using the word parts on page 31. Use each word part once. Your knowledge of word parts, as well as the context clues, will help you create the correct words. If you do not understand the meaning of a word you have made, check your dictionary for the definition or to see if the word exists.

The Job

June was worried about her _____ view. She really needed a job. She sat in the waiting room thinking about her skills. She knew how to behave in a profession_____ manner. She could speak to people on the tele_____ and make them feel like the company cared about them.

She could also _____tate well—she had no problem telling other people what to do.

As she waited in the office, she looked at the other applicants. She could tell one man was very nerv_____. June sym_____ized with him because she felt the same way. June went to sit next to him. She told him that she also _____ liked looking for a job. Milt told her that this was not a situ_____ he enjoyed. Then they smiled at each other and began to _____ lax. They agreed that it was good to feel comfortable again. They liked talking together and realized that it often helps to have someone to _____ fer with to make you feel better or get advice. They hoped they could both get jobs as vice-presidents of the company.

Word Parts

ation	path	phone	inter	re
dic	ous	al	dis	con

4. Pick the best definition of the underlined word. Use your knowledge of word parts to help you determine the definition.

1. The police knew the murder had been <u>premeditated</u> when they found the receipt for the poison dated a week ago.
   a. planned beforehand   b. done again   c. planned with others

2. Her <u>manner</u> was so friendly that I felt relaxed right away at the party.
   a. way of keeping time   b. way of handling things   c. relating to men

3. It was easy to find the <u>anachronism</u> in the picture of the medieval castle: the microwave.
   a. sounding right   b. not at the proper time   c. state of being wrong

4. The student's <u>dramatic</u> presentation caused the class to weep.
   a. relating to drama   b. state of being a drama   c. one who does drama

5. I have to <u>renew</u> my library card; I haven't used it in two years.
   a. to come between   b. to hold one's hand   c. to make new again

6. My new roommate and I are <u>compatible</u>; we both like the same things.
   a. have similar feelings   b. don't speak to each other   c. full of anger

7. Mother <u>intervened</u> when the argument between my brother and me got so serious we were about to hit each other.
   a. stayed away   b. came between   c. knew before

8. The <u>translator</u> had a hard job when everyone spoke at the same time.
   a. one who translates   b. process of translating   c. full of translating

9. I appreciated the <u>congratulation</u> cards from my friends when I passed my driver's test—it took me only six tries.
   a. relating to joy   b. one who expresses joy   c. act of expressing joy

10. If a space shuttle and a planet <u>collide</u>, there will be a huge mess.
    a. to come together with force   b. to stay away from   c. to move in time

CHAPTER 7

Romance

Thank you all for coming this evening. My name is Cathy Leigh. If you look around, you'll see men and women of all ages and backgrounds. Some of you are divorced, others are widowed, and others never married. But you all have something in common. You want to find a better way to **relate** to the opposite sex. First of all, I want to make something perfectly clear: there is nothing wrong with a little flirting. Some of you may think flirting will make you look pushy or **manipulative**. But do you know what? Flirting is a very **harmless** way to get to know other people. It doesn't cost a thing, you can do it anywhere and any time, and it's fun! What more could you want?

Let's take an example. What do you do in a normal day? Go to work, run **errands**, go to the grocery store, the post office, and so on. Well, in each of these places, you have the opportunity to interact with people. What better way to practice the flirting techniques I'm going to give you? Look at the overhead.
 1. Dress to **impress**.
Always look your best. You never know who you'll run into.
 2. **Establish** eye contact.
Get the person to look at you. And smile.
 3. Show **genuine** interest.
Let him or her know that you're really interested.

You see, you never know when or where you're going to meet someone that you find **attractive**, maybe even Mr. or Ms. Right. If you make these techniques part of your everyday life, they'll become second nature. And then, ladies, when you see that handsome hunk, or guys, when you see that **gorgeous** woman that you'd like to get to know, you won't feel **intimidated**—you'll have the confidence to go for it.

A Seminar in Flirting

Predicting

Circle the definition that seems to best fit each vocabulary word. If you have difficulty, return to the reading on page 32, and underline any context clues you find. These clues can help you guess the word's meaning. When you have made your predictions, check your answers against the Word List below. Use the boxes to checkmark those words whose definitions you missed—these are the words you'll want to study closely.

NOTE: You may want to cover the Word List below with a piece of paper so you don't accidentally see the definitions as you do the Predicting exercise.

❏ 1. **relate** (line 6)
   a. to connect
   b. to enjoy
   c. to play

❏ 2. **manipulative** (line 9)
   a. controlling
   b. artistic
   c. selecting

❏ 3. **harmless** (line 10)
   a. safe
   b. dangerous
   c. fun

❏ 4. **errand** (line 14)
   a. adventure
   b. try
   c. routine job

❏ 5. **impress** (line 19)
   a. to influence
   b. to work well
   c. to help

❏ 6. **establish** (line 21)
   a. to express
   b. to stop
   c. to form

❏ 7. **genuine** (line 23)
   a. real
   b. incredible
   c. genius

❏ 8. **attractive** (line 27)
   a. funny
   b. happy
   c. good-looking

❏ 9. **gorgeous** (line 34)
   a. unknown
   b. noble
   c. beautiful

❏ 10. **intimidated** (line 36)
   a. ugly
   b. afraid
   c. sorry

Word List

Word	Part of Speech	Definition
attractive [ə trak′ tiv]	adj.	good-looking
errand [âr′ ənd]	n.	a thing to do; a routine job
establish [e stab′ lish]	v.	to form; to make
genuine [jen′ yōō in]	adj.	real; true
gorgeous [gôr′ jəs]	adj.	beautiful
harmless [härm′ ləs]	adj.	safe; innocent
impress [im pres′]	v.	to influence
intimidated [in tim′ i dā təd]	adj.	scared; frightened
intimidate [in tim′ i dāt]	v.	to scare or frighten
manipulative [mə nip′ yə lā′ tiv] [mə nip′ yə lə tiv]	adj.	using for one's own purposes; controlling
manipulate [mə nip′ yə lāt]	v.	to use for one's own purposes
relate [rē lāt′]	v.	1. to connect 2. to tell or report

Interactive Exercise

Bring a simple drawing that illustrates a vocabulary word from this chapter to your next class. Or, bring a picture from a magazine that illustrates the word, and tape it to this page or to a piece of notebook paper. Underneath the picture, write a sentence with the word used correctly.

The class should then divide into three or four groups. In your group, show your pictures one by one. Group members must try to guess each word.

(Tape or draw picture here.)

Sentence: _____
_____
_____

HINT

When working with others, keep these points in mind:
- Be aware of time limits.
- Give everyone a chance to participate.
- Discover each person's strengths.
- Respect each person's views.
- Have fun.

Self-Tests

> **1** Fill in the blanks with an appropriate word from the list below.

"Hello, Denny? This is Ray. Listen, have I got a story to tell you! Last night I went to this seminar—would you believe me if I tell you I went to a flirting seminar?... Well, yes, because I want to date more and you know how it is sometimes—you see a(n) _____ girl, and you don't know what to do or say. Well, sometimes I just feel _____. I don't suppose you know what that's like, but… (laughter) Okay, this lady named, uh—Cathy Leigh was telling us what to do. She said flirting is _____ because nobody gets hurt or anything. It isn't about being pushy or _____, either. She said you've got to remember three things. Now what were they? Oh, yeah. …she said you should dress to _____. And so even where you're out doing some small _____, you need to look good. Well, at least be clean and have your hair combed! Ha ha! And the second thing was something about trying to get the person to look at you. …What? Oh, yeah, there were girls there—lots of 'em. People of all ages. There was one that was absolutely _____. Did I talk to her? No, but I sure looked at her and she looked at me. You could say we _____ eye contact.…Why not? Well, we didn't learn what to say this time. …Yeah, that comes in part two. Do you wanna go with me next week? Come on now, be a real, _____ friend and go. Maybe we can practice together. Yeah, you help me _____ to women, and I'll help you understand the man's point of view. Is it a deal? Okay, Denise see ya later. Bye."

Vocabulary Words
attractive
relate
gorgeous
errand
impress
established
genuine
harmless
intimidated
manipulative

> **2** True or False? (according to Cathy Leigh, the speaker on page 32)

1. _____ Flirting is usually *manipulative*.

2. _____ You might run into a *gorgeous* person at any time.

3. _____ You should try to look *attractive* when you go out.

4. _____ A lot of people at her seminars feel too *intimidated* to flirt.

5. _____ *Establishing* eye contact isn't important.

6. _____ The right kind of clothes can help you *impress* someone.

7. _____ You could meet Mr. or Ms. Right while you're running *errands*.

8. _____ Never show *genuine* interest; you may look pushy.

9. _____ *Relating* to someone is easier if you know Cathy's techniques.

10. _____ It isn't *harmless* to smile at someone you want to get to know.

CHAPTER

Art

A Day at the Modern Art Museum

Predicting

Circle the definition that seems to best fit each vocabulary word. If you have difficulty, return to the reading on page 36, and underline any context clues you find. These clues can help you guess the word's meaning. When you have made your predictions, check your answers against the Word List below. Use the boxes to checkmark those words whose definitions you missed—these are the words you'll want to study closely.

NOTE: You may want to cover the Word List below with a piece of paper so you don't accidentally see the definitions as you do the Predicting exercise.

☐ 1. **relevance** (panel 1)
   a. unimportance
   b. importance
   c. a curtain

☐ 2. **alienation** (panel 1)
   a. isolation
   b. togetherness
   c. a big party

☐ 3. **symbolize** (panel 2)
   a. to bang
   b. to remember
   c. to represent

☐ 4. **absurdity** (panel 2)
   a. serious
   b. a hard stomach
   c. foolishness

☐ 5. **abstract** (panel 3)
   a. blocked
   b. complex
   c. slim

☐ 6. **desperation** (panel 3)
   a. hopelessness
   b. sweat
   c. happiness

☐ 7. **obviously** (panel 4)
   a. clearly
   b. madly
   c. softly

☐ 8. **futility** (panel 4)
   a. meaningful
   b. meaninglessness
   c. caution

☐ 9. **gallery** (panel 5)
   a. a greenhouse
   b. a kitchen
   c. an exhibition room

☐ 10. **revelation** (panel 6)
   a. a high place
   b. discovery
   c. something confusing

Word List

abstract [ab strakt′]	adj.	disconnected from real life; complex	**gallery** [gal′ ə rē]	n. exhibition room; hall
absurdity [ab sûr′ di tē]	n.	nonsense; foolishness	**obviously** [ob′ vē əs lē]	adv. clearly; plainly
alienation [ā′ lē ə nā′ shən]	n.	division; isolation; distance	**relevance** [rel′ ə vəns]	n. significance; importance
desperation [des′ pə rā′ shən]	n.	hopelessness; sorrow	**revelation** [rev′ ə lā′ shən]	n. announcement; discovery
futility [fyoo til′ ə tē]	n.	emptiness; meaninglessness	**symbolize** [sim′ bə līz′]	v. to represent; to mean

Interactive Exercise

Draw pictures that represent three of the vocabulary words.

Word: _____

Word: _____

Word: _____

Self-Tests

1 Match the situation to the word it best fits.

SET ONE

_____ 1. continuously pushing a rock up a hill and having it roll back   a. alienation

_____ 2. not being friends with anyone   b. revelation

_____ 3. making a connection between a reading in history and a short story in English   c. futility

_____ 4. considering the possibility of time travel   d. relevance

_____ 5. finally understanding how to figure out what *X* is in an equation   e. abstract

SET TWO

_____ 6. a student buying a term paper to pass a class   f. obvious

_____ 7. walking around a place filled with paintings   g. gallery

_____ 8. winking at someone to show you like the person   h. desperation

_____ 9. a college scheduling all classes from midnight to five a.m.   i. symbolize

_____ 10. exchanging rings at a wedding to represent a couple's commitment to each other   j. absurdity

2 You are lost in the art museum, and you ask several people for directions to the gift shop. Put the correct vocabulary words in the spaces below to help you make sense of their answers. Choose from these words: futile, absurd, alienation, abstract, revelation, relevance, desperate, gallery, obviously, symbolize.

"Walk down this _____ to the painting of the woman with three eyes. This complex picture is at the entrance to the _____ collection. Now turn left. Go past two more paintings, and on your right will be a sculpture of a man with his back to you. He is all alone and shows man's _____ in the modern world. As soon as you go by him, turn right, and go downstairs, and you are there."

"You shouldn't have come down these stairs. What kind of _____ instructions did you get? Oh well, don't look so _____; it isn't really that far now. Go back upstairs and turn right. After you pass the big black painting with the blue circle in the middle, which is supposed to _____ the beginning of life (at least that's what the artist told me), you want to turn left and go down those stairs."

"_____, you have been talking to the wrong people, but don't worry. Your search is not _____. Go down this hall and turn left at the picture of the waterfall; you'll understand the _____ of where this painting is placed when you hear the fountain nearby. It's a great effect to put them near each other. Go past the fountain, turn right, and there will be the wonderful _____: the gift shop."

CHAPTER 8   ART   39

CHAPTER 9

Time Management

Elizabeth's Time Management System

ANNOUNCER: This is KHBG Talk Radio, the voice of the city.

RALPH: Good evening, one and all. I'm Ralph Howard, your host. Tonight we have a special program lined up for you. Our guest is Elizabeth Downs, author of the bestseller, *Elizabeth's Time **Management** System.* Elizabeth, welcome to the show.

ELIZABETH: Why, thank you, Ralph. It's a pleasure to be here.

RALPH: Before we open up the phone lines to take questions from our listeners, could you please tell us why you decided to write this book?

ELIZABETH: That's an easy one. I was a very **disorganized** person who never seemed to **accomplish** anything. In spite of my good **intentions**, I always **procrastinated**.

RALPH: You saved things for another day.

ELIZABETH: That's right. But that was before I learned how to **prioritize**. You do things in the order of their importance. The key is keeping a master list of things that you need to do.

RALPH: We have a caller on the line now. Lisa in North Park, are you there?

LISA: Yes. I have a question for Elizabeth. I haven't read your book yet, and I need help. I'm a **frazzled** housewife. I'm tired and frustrated because I'm constantly doing things for my husband and my kids, but I never get the cleaning done.

ELIZABETH: Make a list of all the cleaning jobs in your home. Schedule a day for each of them. The key to this approach is this: Don't give up if you miss a day. Just continue the weekly schedule.

LISA: Oh, thank you!

RALPH: Jerry in Riverside, are you there?

JERRY: Yes, thank you. Elizabeth, I hope you can help me. I'm always late. No matter how early I start something, I never meet my deadlines. I'm just not as **efficient** as I want to be.

ELIZABETH: I'm assuming that you don't have a weekly planner. No? Well, get one. Keep a record of all your appointments. And, once a week sit down and list everything that you need to do. Estimate how much time each **task** will take. Then, decide when you are going to do it. Write it on the planner, and do it. You'll be more **efficient** and **productive** than ever.

Predicting

Circle the definition that seems to best fit each vocabulary word. If you have difficulty, return to the reading on page 40, and underline any context clues you find. These clues can help you guess the word's meaning. When you have made your predictions, check your answers against the Word List below. Use the boxes to checkmark those words whose definitions you missed—these are the words you'll want to study closely.

NOTE: You may want to cover the Word List below with a piece of paper so you don't accidentally see the definitions as you do the Predicting exercise.

☐ 1. **management** (line 4)
   a. decision
   b. employment
   c. control

☐ 2. **disorganized** (line 8)
   a. not in order
   b. dirty
   c. official

☐ 3. **accomplish** (line 9)
   a. to accept
   b. to complete
   c. to regret

☐ 4. **intention** (line 9)
   a. romantic
   b. initiation
   c. plan

☐ 5. **procrastinate** (line 9)
   a. to pass
   b. to postpone
   c. to increase

☐ 6. **prioritize** (line 11)
   a. to put away
   b. to do carefully
   c. to place in order of importance

☐ 7. **frazzled** (line 16)
   a. tired
   b. happy
   c. bored

☐ 8. **efficient** (lines 24 and 28)
   a. admirable
   b. orderly
   c. with effort

☐ 9. **task** (line 27)
   a. order
   b. job
   c. take

☐ 10. **productive** (line 29)
   a. intelligent
   b. completing many jobs
   c. protective

Word List

accomplish
[ə käm′ plish]
v. to complete; to carry out

disorganized
[dis ôr′ gə nīzd′]
adj. not having order

efficient
[ē fish′ ənt, i fish′ ənt]
adj. orderly; effective

frazzled
[fraz′ əld]
adj. tired; exhausted

intention
[in ten′ chən]
n. plan

management
[man′ ij mənt]
n. direction; control

prioritize
[prī ôr′ ə tīz′]
v. to place in order of importance

procrastinate
[pro kras′ tə nāt′]
v. to postpone; to put off

productive
[prə duk′ tiv]
adj. able to complete many jobs

task
[task]
n. assignment; job

Interactive Exercise

Write your answers in one or two sentences. Use a vocabulary word in each answer.

You have applied for a job in **management**. The company will not consider you until you have answered its questionnaire.

HOW ORGANIZED ARE YOU?

1. a. Do you usually *accomplish* your plans or goals outside the office? Why or why not?

   b. Which word describes you more—*efficient* or *disorganized?* Explain.

2. Have you ever felt *frazzled* at work? Describe this.

3. Describe a situation in which you *procrastinated.*

4. Do you use a planner of any type? yes   no
   If so, why do you use it?

   If not, do you think a planner could help you? Explain.

CHAPTER 9   TIME MANAGEMENT

Self-Tests

 Match the description with one of the vocabulary words below.

Vocabulary Words

| productive | efficient | prioritize | intention | disorganized |
| task | frazzled | procrastinate | management | accomplish |

1. _____ I've decided to start a new exercise program.

2. _____ You completed a bachelor's degree with high honors.

3. _____ Jay waits until the last minute to do everything.

4. _____ Brian wrote three books in two years.

5. _____ It's more important to study for my test than watch TV tonight.

6. _____ Betsy never forgets any birthdays or anniversaries.

7. _____ I feel tired and stressed.

8. _____ Wash the clothes.

9. _____ Sandra forgets appointments and loses things.

10. _____ I now have good control of my time.

 For each set, write the letter of the most logical analogy. See appendix for instructions and practice.

SET ONE
1. lose : disorganized :: _____
2. faculty : student :: _____
3. day : night :: _____
4. page : notebook :: _____
5. pencil : writer :: _____

a. task : project
b. find : efficient
c. planner : prioritize
d. fail : accomplish
e. management : secretary

SET TWO
6. few : wasteful :: _____
7. snack : meal :: _____
8. gamble : money :: _____
9. drink : thirst :: _____
10. job: work :: _____

f. disorganized : confused
g. procrastinate : time
h. idea : intention
i. many: productive
j. rest : frazzled

CHAPTER 9 TIME MANAGEMENT

CHAPTER 10

Review: Focus on Chapters 1-9

The following activities give you a chance to interact some more with the vocabulary words you've been learning. By looking at art, acting, writing, taking tests, and doing a crossword puzzle, you will see which words you know well and which you still need to work with.

Art

Match each picture on page 44 to one of the following vocabulary words. Use each word once.

Vocabulary Words

stunning	chorus	scroll	gorgeous	frazzled
campus	chisel	gallery	tome	disorganized
opposition	correspond	triumph	novice	revelation

Drama

Charades: You will be given one of the following words to act out in class. Think about how this word could be demonstrated without speaking. The other people in class will try to guess what word you are showing.

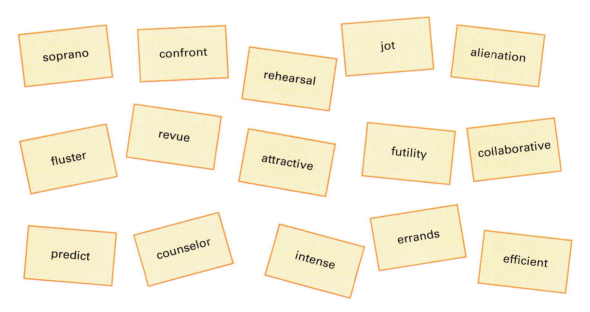

CHAPTER 10 REVIEW 45

Writing

Answer the following questions to further test your understanding of the vocabulary words:

1. Who might need help with phonics? _____

2. What would be an example of a fluke in terms of weather? _____

3. What is something you would have to send in a registration fee for? _____
   _____

4. What are three exciting careers? _____

5. Who on your college's faculty do you really respect? _____

6. What kind of habits are good to establish? _____

7. Where would be a good place to sit and be philosophical? Why? _____
   _____

8. What do you have an aptitude for? _____

9. What are some events that await us at the end of our lives? _____
   _____

10. Where might you expect an orientation? _____

11. Who do you relate well to? _____

12. What would you want to make sure was genuine before you bought it? _____
    _____

13. What might be considered a harmless lie? _____

14. What enchanting place would you like to travel to? _____
    _____

15. What things in your life should you take a yearly assessment of? _____
    _____

Self-Tests

 Finish the story using the vocabulary words below. There will be five words left over.

Learning Words

Matt was _____ about going to college because he did not have a very big vocabulary. His friend Dan, however, told him not to be afraid because he could take a class to build his vocabulary skills. Matt _____ what his friend said, and after thinking about it overnight, he decided he would sign up for the class. He checked to make sure he had not missed the _____ to register. He was in luck and made it with a day to spare.

On the first day the instructor told the class that the semester would not be so _____ if they were willing to study. Matt didn't want to make things hard, so he was ready to spend a lot of time on his assignments. Matt got the book for the class and saw that it was going to be fun to use because it had several _____ exercises. It was great to do activities like art and drama to learn new words. Obviously, he was going to have to _____ himself to his studies, but he would also enjoy it.

One of the techniques Matt learned first was to look for _____. Those were words around a word that could give him an idea of what the word meant. Matt became an _____ at finding these clues. He knew they could come in different forms such as examples, synonyms, or _____. Looking for words that meant the opposite of the word he didn't know was something he had never thought of doing.

On the first quiz Matt got a C. He knew he could have done better if he hadn't _____ and studied only the night before. Matt began a _____ of studying his words every day. He now _____ at least ten hours a week to the class. On the next test and all the rest, Matt got an A.

At the end of the class, Matt had _____ to a lot of new words. He saw his friend Dan one day, who asked for some _____ about how Matt liked the vocabulary class. Matt told him, "I am no longer flustered by the grueling _____ of reading college-level tomes because my vocabulary is now stunning." Dan smiled at his friend and nodded in agreement.

Vocabulary Words

access
antonyms
apply
context clues
deadline
dedicated
expert
feedback
flustered
grueling
intense
interactive
intimidated
obviously
pondered
procrastinated
regimen
revelation
stunning
task

Pick the word that best completes the sentence.

1. I thought I would never finish Aunt Marie's letter; it was like reading a _____.
   a. campus   b. revue   c. tome   d. analogy

2. Wendy looked _____ after a car almost ran into her.
   a. frazzled   b. await   c. genuine   d. grueling

3. The meeting was so _____ no one knew what issue they were voting on.
   a. predicted   b. disorganized   c. pondered   d. intimidated

4. Mom's first marriage came as a _____ to Dad when he got a call from her ex-husband.
   a. expert   b. chisel   c. revelation   d. orientation

5. Marty found skydiving to be an _____ experience; it was extremely exciting.
   a. intense   b. novice   c. confront   d. deadline

6. Jean thought cleaning up after her son was _____ since his room was dirty the next day.
   a. apply   b. prioritize   c. attractive   d. futile

7. Mary was so _____ at doing her homework that she could relax on the weekends.
   a. task   b. efficient   c. alienated   d. gorgeous

8. I don't _____ easily, but when I couldn't find my research paper, I got upset.
   a. procrastinate   b. interactive   c. triumph   d. fluster

9. David had _____ to lots of information after he learned to use the Internet.
   a. access   b. regimen   c. intentions   d. relate

10. There is _____ interest in an English Club. Fifty people showed up for the first meeting.
    a. chorus   b. errand   c. obviously   d. gallery

 HINT
Learn From Your Mistakes

You will be taking quizzes and tests throughout this course, as well as in other classes. Remember that taking a test is simply another way to learn. You learn what you know and what you don't know. When you get a test back, you should always look at your errors, especially if you receive a low grade. It is normal to feel disappointed, but ask yourself first if you really spent enough time with the words before you took the quiz or test. If you didn't, then you will know what you need to do next time. Then, *look at every error.* If you don't understand why something is wrong, ask the teacher. Go back to the chapter and study all of the exercises where the word was used.

If you follow these procedures, you will learn from the error and will probably not make the same mistake again. Keep in mind that *the grade is always less important than what you learn.* If you really learn how to use the words, you'll get good grades.

Crossword Puzzle

Use the following words to complete the crossword puzzle. You will use each word once.

Vocabulary Words

abstract
absurdity
accomplishment
analogy
bass
chisel
collaborative
desperate
diligent
impression
intentions
loathe
major
manager
manipulation
novice
predict
prioritize
productive
relate
relevance
symbolizes
synonyms
task
thematic

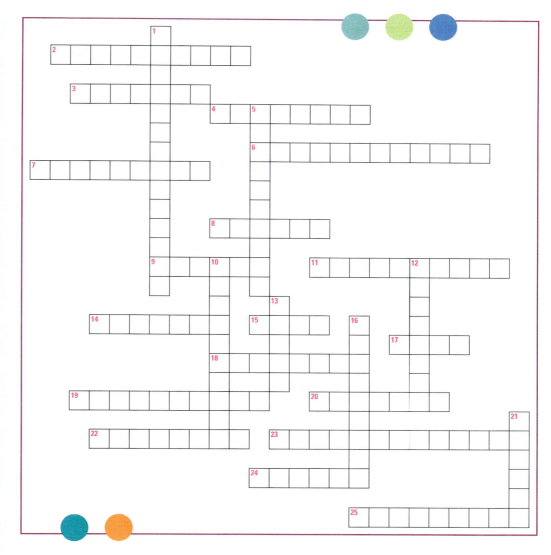

Across
2. to do a lot
3. a comparison
4. a painting by Picasso
6. Tears can be used for this.
7. the strangeness of life
8. a carving tool
9. I have never played tennis.
11. These can be misunderstood.
14. a person in charge
15. a job to do
17. low
18. happy, glad, and cheerful
19. what to do first
20. to tell before it happens
22. The tortoise won the race by being this.
23. We will get it done if we work together.
24. People often feel this way about lima beans and liver.
25. has meaning

Down
1. When I finish my homework, I feel like I have done this.
5. A flag does this for a country.
10. His cooking made this on his girlfriend.
12. a topic
13. for example, English, math, and education
16. People who cheat on a test must be this.
21. feel the same way about something

CHAPTER 10 REVIEW 49

CHAPTER 11

Personalities

As the Cookie Crumbles

How do we know who we are? What the future holds? The answer is simple: we have only to open a fortune cookie to find our true personalities. Do any of these fortunes sound like you?

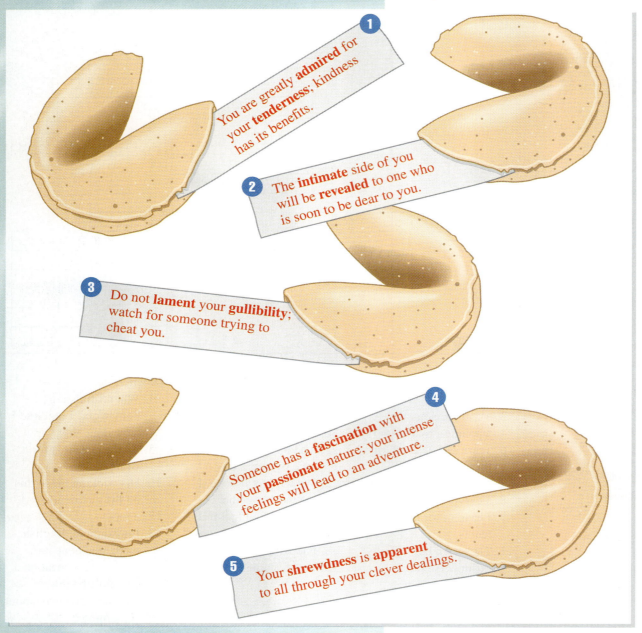

1. You are greatly **admired** for your **tenderness**; kindness has its benefits.

2. The **intimate** side of you will be **revealed** to one who is soon to be dear to you.

3. Do not **lament** your **gullibility**; watch for someone trying to cheat you.

4. Someone has a **fascination** with your **passionate** nature; your intense feelings will lead to an adventure.

5. Your **shrewdness** is **apparent** to all through your clever dealings.

Predicting

Circle the definition that seems to best fit each vocabulary word. If you have difficulty, return to the reading on page 50, and underline any context clues you find. These clues can help you guess the word's meaning. When you have made your predictions, check your answers against the Word List below. Use the boxes to checkmark those words whose definitions you missed—these are the words you'll want to study closely.

NOTE: You may want to cover the Word List below with a piece of paper so you don't accidentally see the definitions as you do the Predicting exercise.

☐ 1. **admire** (fortune 1)
   a. to cry
   b. to think highly of
   c. to get stuck in the mud

☐ 2. **tenderness** (fortune 1)
   a. abandonment
   b. cruelty
   c. warm feelings

☐ 3. **intimate** (fortune 2)
   a. stubborn
   b. formal
   c. of a close, personal nature

☐ 4. **reveal** (fortune 2)
   a. to stop doing
   b. to party
   c. to display

☐ 5. **lament** (fortune 3)
   a. to express grief
   b. to pour concrete
   c. to come near

☐ 6. **gullibility** (fortune 3)
   a. a short trip
   b. the state of believing easily
   c. a kind of bird

☐ 7. **fascination** (fortune 4)
   a. extreme interest
   b. a hook
   c. mismanagement

☐ 8. **passionate** (fortune 4)
   a. old
   b. enthusiastic
   c. bored

☐ 9. **shrewdness** (fortune 5)
   a. an empty area
   b. a small animal
   c. intelligence

☐ 10. **apparent** (fortune 5)
   a. courageous
   b. clear
   c. mom or dad

Word List

admire [ad mīʳrʹ]	v.	to think highly of	**lament** [lə mentʹ]	v. to express grief
apparent [ə parʹ ənt, ə pârʹ-]	adj.	easily seen or understood; clear; evident	**passionate** [pashʹ ən it]	adj. having strong emotions; enthusiastic; loving
fascination [fasʹ ə nāʹ shən]	n.	extreme interest; enchantment	**reveal** [ri vēlʹ]	v. to make known; to display
gullibility [gulʹ ə bilʹ i tē]	n.	the state of believing too easily and therefore being easily fooled	**shrewdness** [shroodʹ nis]	n. intelligence; common sense
intimate [inʹ tə mit]	adj.	of a very close, personal, or private nature	**tenderness** [tenʹ dər nes]	n. warm feelings; softness

Interactive Exercise

Imagine that you write fortunes for cookies. Using the vocabulary words, complete the first fortunes, and then write two of your own.

Your _____ toward a friend will _____ a surprising secret.

Your _____ with the stars will lead to a _____ affair.

People _____ you for your _____ in business.

Self-Tests

 Match the word to the situation it best fits.

SET ONE

_____ 1. Barbara is crying over her dog's death. a. lament

_____ 2. When the monster took off his mask, we were surprised to discover James. b. reveal

_____ 3. Sara told Josefina about a recurring dream that was frightening her. c. tenderness

_____ 4. The little boy stares at a fish tank for hours. d. intimate

_____ 5. Belinda put her arm around her nervous little sister as they entered school the first day. e. fascination

> **HINT**
>
> Study anywhere and anytime you can! If you have only ten minutes while you're waiting for something, use that time to study a little. It would be better to study your vocabulary words five different times for ten minutes each time than to study only one time for an hour!

SET TWO

_____ 6. The man turned a $50 investment into $5,000. f. apparent

_____ 7. Mike's brother knocked on the door and ran away six times; his brother got up to answer it every time. g. admire

_____ 8. The math major stayed up all night solving equations, and he wanted more. h. gullibility

_____ 9. Barney shook his teacher's hand at the end of the semester and thanked her for all she had taught him. i. passionate

_____ 10. Mom and Dad came home and saw the pile of paper plates in the trash and the soda stains on the rug; they knew there had been a party. j. shrewdness

2 Fill in the blanks with the appropriate vocabulary words. Remember to use context clues to help you. Use each word once.

1. Teachers _____ students who study hard. They regard these students highly because they see the pride the students feel for themselves.

2. It is _____ that you like to eat Chinese food; you have gone to four Chinese restaurants this week.

3. A _____ student will be enthusiastic about studying.

4. She shared the most _____ details of her love life with her best friend.

5. The student showed his _____ when he took the time to study instead of going to the party.

6. He was afraid to _____ his true feelings about loving to cook because his father thought it was something only women did.

7. After he failed the test, the student _____ going to the party instead of studying.

8. My _____ with the stars led me to take an astronomy class.

9. Because of the student's _____, he believed the teacher when she said, "I like it when students come to class unprepared." The next day he felt foolish when he didn't bring his textbook.

10. The mother's _____ toward her baby was easy to see when she hugged him.

Vocabulary Words

admire
tenderness
intimate
reveal
lamented
gullibility
fascination
passionate
shrewdness
apparent

CHAPTER 11 PERSONALITIES

CHAPTER 12

History

Cleopatra's Diary

The Times

Priceless Manuscript Uncovered in Egypt

(Cairo AP) A team of **archaeologists** has made a discovery that appears to be one of the most **remarkable** in recorded history. According to Professor James Elliot of the University of Chicago, who has directed the exploration, a papyrus **manuscript** was discovered yesterday in a previously **uncharted** tunnel of an ancient tomb. Due to security reasons, the exact location has not been **disclosed**. **Preliminary** examination indicates that the manuscript is approximately two thousand years old. Dr. Friedrich von Hoffman, an expert in **hieroglyphics**, announced that the manuscript appears to be a diary containing details of the life of Queen Cleopatra VII, possibly written by personal scribes. Von Hoffman stated that events recorded in the document are ordered **chronologically** and appear historically **accurate**.

Steps have already been taken to preserve as well as to ensure the **authenticity** of the ancient document, which has become the property of the Egyptian Bureau of Antiquities.

Predicting

Circle the definition that seems to best fit each vocabulary word. If you have difficulty, return to the reading on page 54, and underline any context clues you find. These clues can help you guess the word's meaning. When you have made your predictions, check your answers against the Word List below. Use the boxes to checkmark those words whose definitions you missed—these are the words you'll want to study closely.

NOTE: You may want to cover the Word List below with a piece of paper so you don't accidentally see the definitions as you do the Predicting exercise.

❑ 1. **archaeologists** (line 1)
   a. antique dealers
   b. language experts
   c. scientists who study ancient ways of life

❑ 2. **remarkable** (line 4)
   a. fantastic
   b. fanatic
   c. ordinary

❑ 3. **manuscript** (line 8)
   a. typed paper
   b. handwritten document
   c. fake document

❑ 4. **uncharted** (line 10)
   a. undecided
   b. unreachable
   c. never explored

❑ 5. **disclose** (line 13)
   a. make public
   b. keep private
   c. diagnose

❑ 6. **preliminary** (line 14)
   a. quick
   b. beginning
   c. preventive

❑ 7. **hieroglyphics** (line 18)
   a. ancient music
   b. ancient art form
   c. ancient form of writing

❑ 8. **chronological** (line 27)
   a. mathematical order
   b. spatial order
   c. in time order

❑ 9. **accurate** (line 29)
   a. correct
   b. ancient
   c. incorrect

❑ 10. **authenticity** (line 35)
   a. age
   b. quality
   c. realness

Word List

accurate [akʹ yŭr it]	*adj.*	correct; exact	**disclose** [dis klōzʹ]	*v.*	to make public
archaeologist [ärʹ kē älʹ ə jist]	*n.*	one who studies the remains of past human life	**hieroglyphics** [hīʹ rō glifʹ iks]	*n.*	pictorial writing system used in ancient Egypt
archaeology [ärʹ kē olʹ ə jē]	*n.*	the scientific study of the remains of past human life	**manuscript** [manʹ yoo skript]	*n.*	document, generally handwritten
authenticity [ôʹ then tisʹ ə tē]	*n.*	realness; genuineness	**preliminary** [pre limʹ ə närʹ ē]	*adj.*	beginning; introductory
authentic [ô thenʹ tik]	*adj.*	real	**remarkable** [rē märʹ kə bəl]	*adj.*	great; incredible
chronological [kronʹ ə loʹ ji kəl]	*adj.*	arranged in order of time; sequential	**uncharted** [un chärʹ təd]	*adj.*	unexplored

Interactive Exercise

ANTONYMS

Write a vocabulary word next to the sentence with a word or phrase that is most nearly its *opposite*.

1. _____ Their conversation was very *ordinary*.

2. _____ The story he gave was *not in the proper time sequence*.

3. _____ My aunt believed the lamp at the antique show was a *fake*.

4. _____ Our state has been completely *explored and mapped*.

5. _____ The local police will *not tell* who gave them the information.

6. _____ An *investigator of future human life* was recently interviewed on CNN.

7. _____ Perhaps someday someone will invent an *easy writing system*.

8. _____ Our vacation plans are in the *final* stages.

9. _____ Everything she told us was *wrong*.

10. _____ Mary's novel has been *published*.

Vocabulary Words
archaeologists
remarkable
manuscript
uncharted
disclose
preliminary
hieroglyphics
chronological
accurate
authentic

Self-Tests

1 Fill in the blanks with one of the vocabulary words listed on page 57.

Human beings are constantly finding new ways of exploring _____ territory. On _____ examination, some things appear impossible to do. It is _____ that so many advances and discoveries have been made. However, new findings are not usually _____ to the public until they have been tested for their _____.

In Egypt in the year 1799, French troops led by Napoleon found a stone slab, which was called the Rosetta Stone. Greek and other languages appeared on the stone with the ancient Egyptian _____. Not only _____, but the rest of the world was very excited about this incredible discovery. The stone provided a(n) _____ translation

CHAPTER 12 HISTORY

of the ancient Egyptian writing system. As a result of this discovery, it is easier to understand the _____ order of events in the ancient world. Perhaps one day a handwritten _____ or another stone will be found, telling us more about the ancient world—maybe even a diary belonging to Cleopatra.

Vocabulary Words
archaeologists
remarkable
manuscript
uncharted
disclosed
preliminary
hieroglyphics
chronological
accurate
authenticity

2 Match the vocabulary word with the correct definition.

1. _____ manuscript
2. _____ preliminary
3. _____ accurate
4. _____ chronological
5. _____ authenticity
6. _____ remarkable
7. _____ archaeologist
8. _____ disclose
9. _____ hieroglyphics
10. _____ uncharted

a. correct
b. in order of time
c. undiscovered
d. beginning
e. ancient form of writing
f. unbelievable
g. make public
h. one who studies remains of human history
i. realness
j. document

CHAPTER  13

Politics

Be a Good American—VOTE!

Predicting

Circle the definition that seems to best fit each vocabulary word. If you have difficulty, return to the reading on page 58, and underline any context clues you find. These clues can help you guess the word's meaning. When you have made your predictions, check your answers against the Word List below. Use the boxes to checkmark those words whose definitions you missed—these are the words you'll want to study closely.

NOTE: You may want to cover the Word List below with a piece of paper so you don't accidentally see the definitions as you do the Predicting exercise.

☐ 1. **ballot** (panel 1)
   a. a song
   b. a piece of wood to cut on
   c. a form for voting

☐ 2. **verify** (panel 2)
   a. to make certain that something is correct
   b. to make certain that something is foreign
   c. to help someone

☐ 3. **identity** (panel 2)
   a. a twin
   b. a certain person
   c. a god

☐ 4. **absentee** (panel 2)
   a. not physically present
   b. not mentally alert
   c. a type of beverage

☐ 5. **polls** (panel 3)
   a. a thing to hang a flag on
   b. a place where people vote
   c. a skunk

☐ 6. **inconvenience** (panel 3)
   a. a type of store
   b. not able to be comforted
   c. troublesome occurrence

☐ 7. **queues** (panel 3)
   a. a dock
   b. a type of hairdo
   c. people waiting in lines

☐ 8. **proxy** (panel 3)
   a. a woman's name
   b. a stand-in
   c. a type of bleach

☐ 9. **candidates** (panel 4)
   a. nice people to go out with
   b. people who want to be elected to office
   c. food

☐ 10. **proposition** (panel 4)
   a. offers for change
   b. a part of speech
   c. a type of candy

Word List

absentee
[ab′ sən tē′]
n. a person who is not present

ballot
[bal′ ət]
n. a form or paper used for voting

candidates
[kan′ di dāts, kan′ di dits]
n. people who are trying to get elected into office

identity
[ī den′ ti tē′, i den′ ti tē]
n. a certain person or thing

inconvenience
[in′ kən vēn′ yəns]
n. a troublesome occurrence that does not meet one's needs

polls
[pōls]
n. a place where people go to vote

proposition
[prop′ ə zish′ ən]
n. a plan or offer that is up for approval

proxy
[prok′ sē]
n. a person who is approved to act for someone who is not present

queues
[kyōōz]
n. lines of people waiting for something

verify
[vâr′ ə fī′]
v. to say definitely that something is correct

Interactive Exercise

For each topic or category give three examples.

Situations where a ballot is used:
1. _____
2. _____
3. _____

Things that may be done by proxy:
1. _____
2. _____
3. _____

Inconveniences you've known:
1. _____
2. _____
3. _____

Where your identity may be questioned:
1. _____
2. _____
3. _____

Things that must be verified:
1. _____
2. _____
3. _____

Places where you've seen queues:
1. _____
2. _____
3. _____

Self-Tests

 Use the vocabulary words to fill in the blanks.

I think it is a major _____ when I go somewhere and then have to stand in a line. When I see a _____ of people waiting, I try to find a way to avoid that situation. Why not pay homeless people to wait in line for other people? They could act as _____ for people who have more money than time. It would create a situation where _____ waiting would be helpful for everyone. The only problem I can see with my idea is that the _____ of the person being waited for by proxy would have to be checked (_____) so that the homeless person would not be tempted to wait for more than one person at a time. That way more homeless people could be employed, one for each person who didn't want to wait.

This is a great plan! I'm going to make it into a _____ that voters can consider at the next election. Just think: When people go to the _____ they'll be looking at my proposition! They'll cast a _____ for or against my plan. It's always fun to have lots of new ideas to vote on along with the _____ we elect to office each year.

Vocabulary Words
absentee
ballot
candidates
identity
inconvenience
polls
propositions
proxies
queue
verified

Match the vocabulary word to the situation that suggests the word.

____ 1. It was too long, so I left.

____ 2. It got stuck in the machine that counts them.

____ 3. I went there to vote, but it had already closed.

____ 4. I wanted to pay by check, so I showed my I.D.

____ 5. The officer looked closely at my photo, then at my face.

____ 6. I had to leave home three hours early because the bank is open only when I'm at work.

____ 7. I got that kind of ballot because I didn't have time to go in to vote on Election Day.

____ 8. It's how my brother got married because he was in Korea on the day of his wedding, but his bride was in Alaska.

____ 9. I don't know how these people can handle the stories about them in the press, the difficult schedule, and the expense of trying to be elected.

____ 10. These are the most difficult parts to read on the ballot because they are written in legal words. It's almost as if no one wants the voters to understand these proposals.

Vocabulary Words
a. absentee
b. ballot
c. candidate
d. identity
e. inconvenience
f. polls
g. propositions
h. proxy
i. queue
j. verified

> **HINT**
>
> Studies have shown that it is better to study before you go to sleep and then wait about two to four hours after you wake up to study again. We produce a hormone during our sleep that keeps us from effectively remembering new information! It's better to study when that hormone is out of our bodies, two to four hours after we wake up.

CHAPTER 14

Friendship

Dear Sheila,

You've always been one of my most **supportive** friends. You've given me **sympathy** and comfort when my love life wasn't going exactly the way that I wanted. We've had a
5 few **rifts** over the years, but we've always been able to **compromise** in order to remain friends. I've always trusted you to keep **confidential** things I tell you in private. You've never been one of those people who enjoy gossiping. Especially **malicious gossip** just isn't your style.
10 You always try to **empathize** with my situation when I've sought your counsel, then share your sound **advice**. It's because you've been such a **loyal** and true friend that I'd like to ask if you'll be a bridesmaid at my wedding to Mike in June. I know that you'll have to come five
15 hundred miles, but I hope that you will be able to come.

Love,
Sherry

Predicting

Circle the definition that seems to best fit each vocabulary word. If you have difficulty, return to the reading on page 62, and underline any context clues you find. These clues can help you guess the word's meaning. When you have made your predictions, check your answers against the Word List below. Use the boxes to checkmark those words whose definitions you missed—these are the words you'll want to study closely.

NOTE: You may want to cover the Word List below with a piece of paper so you don't accidentally see the definitions as you do the Predicting exercise.

❑ 1. **supportive** (line 2)
   a. fun
   b. encouraging
   c. holding up a person's body weight

❑ 2. **sympathy** (line 3)
   a. presents
   b. showing understanding
   c. showing playfulness

❑ 3. **rifts** (line 5)
   a. breaks
   b. good jokes
   c. good parties

❑ 4. **compromise** (line 6)
   a. to hurt
   b. to disagree
   c. to agree by giving up part of your opinion

❑ 5. **confidential** (line 7)
   a. announced in public
   b. about the whole world
   c. secret

❑ 6. **malicious** (line 9)
   a. not good smelling
   b. good tasting
   c. meant to hurt someone

❑ 7. **gossip** (line 9)
   a. information that may be untrue
   b. running fast
   c. swallowing fast

❑ 8. **empathize** (line 10)
   a. to understand another's feelings
   b. to kill humanely
   c. to help

❑ 9. **advice** (line 11)
   a. a type of word part
   b. an opinion about how to act
   c. a bad habit

❑ 10. **loyal** (line 12)
   a. true to someone or something
   b. harmful
   c. helpful

Word List

advice [ad vīs′] *n.* an opinion about how to act

compromise [kom′ prə mīz] *v.* to agree by giving up part of what you want

confidential [kän′ fə den′ chəl] *adj.* spoken or written for only a few people to know about; secret

empathize [em′ pə thīz] *v.* to identify with another person's situation; to understand his or her feelings

gossip [gäs′ əp] *n.* 1. information that may be untrue, especially about other people
2. a person who gives information that may be untrue

loyal [loi′ əl] *adj.* not changing in one's devotion to a person, cause, or country

malicious [mə lish′ əs] *adj.* feeling or showing a desire to harm another

rift [rift] *n.* a break or crack

supportive [sə pôr′ tiv] *adj.* giving strength and encouragement

sympathy [sim′ pə thē] *n.* a feeling of tenderness for another person's pain

Interactive Exercise

Write an answer to Sherry's letter, using as many vocabulary words as you can.

Dear _____,

_____

Self-Tests

1 Here are some general headings:

a. good advice
b. give empathy
c. keep this confidential
d. poor advice
e. gossip
f. give sympathy
g. malicious gossip

Match the general headings above with the quotes below:

_____ 1. "Gary and Joan are dating."

_____ 2. "My father passed away last week."

_____ 3. "Call in sick for the rest of the week; then maybe they'll appreciate you!"

_____ 4. "Juanita never does as much work as the rest of us; she's lazy. I'm going to make sure that our boss knows about it."

_____ 5. "Everyone laughed at me when I asked that question. I felt dumb!"

_____ 6. "Be on time!"

_____ 7. "I heard the company is expanding. We'll all be making $1,000 more a month!"

_____ 8. "I wanted to look so good, but this face-lift just made me look surprised!"

_____ 9. "I'm going to quit this job, but don't tell the boss!"

_____ 10. "You know that Maria is fighting with John again. Their marriage is in trouble. I'm going to tell his ex-girlfriend that she should try to get him back!"

Use the clues to fill in the blanks with the individual letters of vocabulary words. When you've completed the horizontal words, a vertical word will be revealed.

10.

1. _ _ _ _ _ _ _ _
2. _ _ _ _ _ _
3. _ _ _ _ _ _ _ _ _ _
4. _ _ _ _ _
5. _ _ _ _ _ _ _ _ _
6. _ _ _ _
7. _ _ _ _ _
8. _ _ _ _ _ _ _ _
9. _ _ _ _ _ _ _

CLUES

1. to understand because you've had the same experience
2. an opinion given about future behavior
3. should not be told to everyone; secret
4. you might like to pass this on, but don't want it to mention you
5. to meet someone halfway in making an agreement
6. We hate it when these develop in our relationships.
7. true to someone or something
8. to give comfort and encouragement
9. a feeling of tenderness toward another's misfortune
10. _____ (You write the clue!)

CHAPTER 14   FRIENDSHIP   65

CHAPTER 15

Travel

Jae Yoon's Big Adventure

Jae Yoon was excited because his trip to New York City was fast **approaching**. He had **estimated** his **expenses**, and he would have enough money if he followed his **budget**. He had made his **reservations** for the plane and hotel. Everything was ready.

When Jae Yoon got to the airport, he checked the **timetable** to see what gate his plane was leaving from. Once he was on the plane, Jae Yoon pulled out his guidebook and marveled at all the **sightseeing** he could do. He just hoped he could fit in all the **excursions** he had planned, such as a trip to the Trade Center, the United Nations, and the Museum of Modern Art. He also had to leave time to buy **souvenirs** for his friends. Many people requested t-shirts showing the Empire State Building or the Statue of Liberty.

When the flight **attendant** came by with the drinks, he told Jae Yoon, "You are going to love New York. It is an exciting city with a lot to do."

Jae Yoon replied, "It looks like there is too much to do."

"No matter what you do, I guarantee you will have a great time."

Jae Yoon smiled and thought the attendant was right. He then took a nap and dreamed of his arrival in the Big Apple.

Predicting

Circle the definition that seems to best fit each vocabulary word. If you have difficulty, return to the reading on page 66, and underline any context clues you find. These clues can help you guess the word's meaning. When you have made your predictions, check your answers against the Word List below. Use the boxes to checkmark those words whose definitions you missed—these are the words you'll want to study closely.

NOTE: You may want to cover the Word List below with a piece of paper so you don't accidentally see the definitions as you do the Predicting exercise.

☐ 1. **approaching** (line 2)
   a. scolding
   b. coming near
   c. leaving

☐ 2. **estimate** (line 2)
   a. to hint
   b. to think highly of
   c. to judge the value or amount

☐ 3. **expenses** (line 2)
   a. past thoughts
   b. something for free
   c. the amount spent on something

☐ 4. **budget** (line 3)
   a. a small plane
   b. a kind of bird
   c. the amount of money or time devoted to a purpose

☐ 5. **reservation** (line 3)
   a. a difference
   b. a held seat or room
   c. the amount promised

☐ 6. **timetable** (line 5)
   a. a schedule
   b. an old clock
   c. a place for breakfast

☐ 7. **sightseeing** (line 7)
   a. looking over a paper
   b. making a mess
   c. visiting places of interest

☐ 8. **excursion** (line 8)
   a. a short trip
   b. a former dog hater
   c. a place to shop

☐ 9. **souvenir** (line 10)
   a. a weapon
   b. a French coin
   c. an item bought as a reminder of a trip

☐ 10. **attendant** (line 13)
   a. a person who sleeps late
   b. a person who asks many questions
   c. a person whose duty is to provide a service

Word List

approach [ə prōch'] v. to come near

attendant [ə ten' dənt] n. a person whose duty is to provide a service

budget [buj' it] n. the amount of money or time devoted to a purpose

estimate [es' tə māt'] v. to judge the approximate amount of something
[es' tə mit] n. a judgment of something's approximate amount

excursion [ik skûr' zhən] n. a short trip

expenses [ek spen' səz] n. the amount spent in doing something

reservation [rez' ər vā' shən] n. 1. a reserved seat or accommodation
2. a reluctance to do something; a doubt

sightseeing [sīt' sē' ing] n. visiting places of interest

souvenir [soō' və nēr'] n. something bought as a reminder of a trip

timetable [tīm' tā' bəl] n. 1. a list showing arrivals and departures of various types of transportation
2. a schedule showing the times of certain activities

Interactive Exercise

LET'S TRAVEL

Time for a mini-vacation is fast *approaching,* and you need to make plans now. You have three days and $300 to spend. Decide where you would like to go, and prepare the following items:

1. *Estimate* your *expenses* for each day.

   food _____   transportation _____

   lodging _____   excursions _____

   souvenirs _____

2. *Budget* your time by making a *timetable* for each day; mention what *sightseeing* you will do.

	Day 1	Day 2	Day 3
morning	_____	_____	_____
afternoon	_____	_____	_____
evening	_____	_____	_____

3. What kind of things do you have to make *reservations* for? Will you need to tip any *attendants?*

4. What kind of *souvenirs* will you likely buy?

Self-Tests

> **1** Finish the story using the vocabulary words on page 69. Use each word once.

Jae Yoon's Trip Back

It was time for Jae Yoon to go home. His _____ were just what he had planned, and he had used up all his money. He had also _____ his time well and had seen everything he wanted. Of all the _____ he took, Jae Yoon's favorite was to the Statue of Liberty. He had bought a lot of _____ there for his friends and himself. He especially liked the torch that was a nightlight. Jae Yoon looked over his

_____ once more before going to bed. He _____ that he had two hours left in the morning for any more visits, and then it was time to go to the airport. He decided that his final _____ would be a walk through Central Park to watch the people of New York City.

The next day when Jae Yoon was getting on the bus, he surprisingly saw the _____ from his flight over walking toward him. As the attendant _____, he recognized Jae Yoon.

He asked, "Will you have any _____ in recommending a visit to New York to your friends? "

Jae Yoon smiled and replied, "I don't have one doubt—they should all come here. I love New York!"

Vocabulary Words

| approached | estimated | budgeted | excursions | expenses |
| reservations | timetable | attendant | souvenirs | sightseeing |

2. Match the quotation to the word it best illustrates. Use each word once.

1. "Do you have any rooms available on November 22?" _____

2. "How much time did you allow for your homework this weekend?" _____

3. "I am guessing that there should be about one hundred people at the reunion." _____

4. "I got you this lovely cuckoo clock from my trip to Germany." _____

5. "Today I am going to visit the Washington Monument, the Jefferson Memorial, and the White House." _____

6. "Thank you for using our parking service. I'll be right back with your car." _____

7. "Did you see when our train is supposed to leave?" _____

8. "Did you enjoy the day trip to see the art museum?" _____

9. "Going to the fair costs a lot; I've spent money on food, jewelry, and rides." _____

10. "Our departure time is getting close." _____

Vocabulary Words

estimate
approaching
budget
expenses
attendant
timetable
reservation
excursion
sightseeing
souvenir

CHAPTER 16

Pets

The Dachshund Memorial Page

The Dachshund Memorial Page

Greta, you were always my baby. I still can't believe you're gone. When I came home from work every day you always greeted me with your **unbridled** affection and noisy, joyful barks. I would pet you, and you showered me with your sweet canine kisses. You sat up so **nobly**, in true dachshund style. You seemed almost human at times. Often, you would look at me and I knew what you wanted, and you seemed to understand how I felt. If I felt sad, you comforted me; when I was happy, you shared that, too. You have been and always will be a **vital** part of our family.

I'll never forget the day we adopted you. We had lost our other dachsie the year before, and we wanted to find another puppy. You were so **clumsy** as you ran around the yard, trying to keep up with the others in your dachsund family. You were the smallest of the litter, but your **invincible** spirit could be seen even then. Greta, you were a fighter. You went with us on long car trips, and you protected us from strangers. And, somehow you even managed to get over your discomfort when we adopted another dachshund puppy, five years ago. At first you took this as an **affront**, but then Petey became your constant companion. Now he doesn't quite know what to do with himself.

You'll always be in our hearts, Greta, and we'll never forget how you refused to give up even after the doctor gave us the **prognosis** that you had terminal cancer. You were loyal and loving to the end, even though I know you were suffering. Then one sad morning we found that you had quietly passed away in your sleep. Now we're trying to **cope** with our **bereavement**. I wrote these words for your **epitaph**:

Greta
1988–1998
Beloved by Mom, Ben, & Petey.
A truly noble dog who will
ever remain in our hearts.
We shall meet you
on the rainbow bridge.

Predicting

Circle the definition that seems to best fit each vocabulary word. If you have difficulty, return to the reading on page 70, and underline any context clues you find. These clues can help you guess the word's meaning. When you have made your predictions, check your answers against the Word List below. Use the boxes to checkmark those words whose definitions you missed—these are the words you'll want to study closely.

NOTE: You may want to cover the Word List below with a piece of paper so you don't accidentally see the definitions as you do the Predicting exercise.

☐ 1. **unbridled** (line 4)
   a. very funny
   b. not controlled
   c. loud

☐ 2. **nobly** (line 5)
   a. showing admirable manners
   b. showing knees
   c. showing patience

☐ 3. **vital** (line 8)
   a. vitamin
   b. hungry
   c. important

☐ 4. **clumsy** (line 10)
   a. silly
   b. showing difficulty in moving
   c. showing power

☐ 5. **invincible** (line 12)
   a. not defeatable
   b. easily beaten
   c. vehicle

☐ 6. **affront** (line 15)
   a. in front
   b. insult
   c. jump

☐ 7. **prognosis** (line 18)
   a. presentation
   b. sickness
   c. chance of recovery

☐ 8. **cope** (line 20)
   a. bury
   b. stop
   c. survive

☐ 9. **bereavement** (line 21)
   a. period of sadness
   b. management
   c. breathing

☐ 10. **epitaph** (line 21)
   a. scrapbook
   b. puppies
   c. statement in memory of the dead

Word List

affront [ə frunt′] — *n.* insult; *v.* to insult

bereavement [bē rēv′ mənt] — *n.* period of mourning following a death

clumsy [klum′ zē] — *adj.* moving with difficulty; awkward

cope [kōp] — *v.* to survive; to manage

epitaph [ep′ i taf′] — *n.* brief statement in memory of the dead, usually on a gravestone

invincible [in vin′ sə bəl] — *adj.* unconquerable; undefeatable

nobly [nō′ blē] — *adv.* admirably; in a dignified way

noble [nō′ bəl] — *adj.* admirable

prognosis [präg nō′ sis] — *n.* medical prediction about chances of survival

unbridled [un brīd′ əld] — *adj.* free; unrestricted

vital [vīt′ əl] — *adj.* essential; important

Interactive Exercise

The reading in this chapter is about a dog, but in this activity, think about other animals.

1. What animal(s) would you never want to *affront*?
   _____

2. What kinds of animals *cope* well

   a. as a pet in a small living area?
   _____

   b. living and hunting alone?
   _____

3. What kind of animal can you picture as *unbridled*? Explain why.
   _____

4. Consider animals living in the wild.

   a. Which do you think is the most *invincible*?
   _____

   b. Which is the most *noble*?
   _____

   c. Which is the most *clumsy*?
   _____

5. The words written in memory of Greta express feelings of *bereavement*, because the dog was a *vital* part of this family. What is your opinion of this attitude toward animals? Use vocabulary words in your answer.
   _____
   _____

Self-Tests

1 Which of the vocabulary words below lends itself to each description?

1. walking when you first wake up _____
2. your heart beating _____
3. saving lives during a disaster _____
4. wearing black _____
5. someone ignoring you after you say hello _____
6. a doctor telling you how long you will live _____
7. thinking that nothing can hurt you _____
8. running wild and free _____
9. reading at the cemetery _____
10. getting through a difficult situation _____

Vocabulary Words
unbridled
cope
epitaph
noble
invincible
prognosis
bereavement
clumsy
affront
vital

2 Circle the word that best completes the sentence.

1. The family wasn't ready for their sad (affront, bereavement) when their dog died.
2. Thinking that they might see their pet again in the next life—on the "Rainbow Bridge"—helps people to (unbridle, cope) with a pet's death.
3. Greta, a dachshund, had (noble, clumsy) qualities that seemed human to her family.
4. A(n) (epitaph, bereavement) was written for Greta.
5. Pets are a (prognosis, vital) part of some people's lives.
6. Animals don't care about showing their (unbridled, coping) feelings.
7. A fighter tries to be (prognosis, invincible).
8. A veterinarian, an animal doctor, gave Greta a (vital, prognosis) of a month.
9. Some animals are (noble, clumsy); others move easily.
10. If they do not get attention, people and animals may take it as an (unbridle, affront).

CHAPTER 16 PETS

CHAPTER 17

The Environment

Environmental **Awareness** Club Forming

First Meeting Wednesday, Sept. 16, at 3 P.M. in room 200

5   **Come find out about environmental problems:**

Depletion of the ozone layer—less ozone equals more of the sun's harmful rays
Global Warming—getting hotter everywhere may lead to melting icecaps and flooding
Endangered Species— the **trend** of building houses and farming where animals once lived means the possible loss of some kinds of animals

10   To **stimulate** interest in environmental causes
we will ask members to decide what to do first—
come help us establish our priority for the year

Our motto: *If everyone **cooperates** the Earth **benefits***

Join us in making the world a better place by becoming an **avid** member
15   Bring your enthusiasm and arrive early
We **anticipate** a full room
Refreshments will be served

74

Predicting

Circle the definition that seems to best fit each vocabulary word. If you have difficulty, return to the reading on page 75, and underline any context clues you find. These clues can help you guess the word's meaning. When you have made your predictions, check your answers against the Word List below. Use the boxes to checkmark those words whose definitions you missed—these are the words you'll want to study closely.

NOTE: You may want to cover the Word List below with a piece of paper so you don't accidentally see the definitions as you do the Predicting exercise.

❑ 1. **awareness** (line 1)
   a. fear
   b. knowledge
   c. state of exhaustion

❑ 2. **depletion** (line 6)
   a. increase
   b. reduction
   c. abundance

❑ 3. **global** (line 7)
   a. bright
   b. healthy
   c. international

❑ 4. **endangered** (line 8)
   a. glowing
   b. not mad
   c. the possibility of extinction

❑ 5. **trend** (line 8)
   a. a form
   b. a general direction
   c. a dependable person

❑ 6. **stimulate** (line 10)
   a. to excite
   b. to enlist
   c. to hurt

❑ 7. **cooperate** (line 13)
   a. to work together
   b. to disagree
   c. to remove

❑ 8. **benefit** (line 13)
   a. advantage
   b. crumb
   c. disadvantage

❑ 9. **avid** (line 14)
   a. depressed
   b. enthusiastic
   c. foaming

❑ 10. **anticipate** (line 16)
   a. to fear
   b. to join in
   c. to expect

Word List

anticipate [an tis′ ə pāt′]	v. to look forward to; to expect	**endangered** [en dān′ jûrd]	adj. the possibility of extinction (to no longer be)
avid [av′ id]	adj. eager; enthusiastic	**endanger** [en dān′ jər]	v. to expose to danger
awareness [ə wâr′ nes]	n. consciousness; knowledge	**global** [glō′ bəl]	adj. involving the entire Earth; international
benefit [ben′ ə fit]	n. anything that helps well-being; advantage	**stimulate** [stim′ yə lāt′]	v. to excite; to inspire; to cause to do
cooperate [kō äp′ ər āt]	v. to work together; to agree	**trend** [trend]	n. a general direction in which something tends to move; a leaning
depletion [di plē′ shən]	n. the act of decreasing something; reduction		

CHAPTER 17 THE ENVIRONMENT

Interactive Exercise

Below is a chapter from an imaginary textbook about the environment. Complete the exercises to gain practice in using the vocabulary words.

The Environment and You   Lesson I

What do you know about the environment? Test your environmental *awareness* by answering the following questions. These matters will be discussed in the rest of the text.

Exercise I. List two *global* environmental problems. Example: *depletion* of forests worldwide

1. _____   2. _____

Exercise II. *Endangered* species is one problem society faces. List three endangered animals you think the Earth might lose.

1. _____   2. _____   3. _____

Exercise III. List ways you can *stimulate* people to become *avid* environmentalists. Think about current *trends,* such as recycling, to develop your list.

1. _____   2. _____   3. _____

Self-Tests

1 Write the vocabulary word on the line below the situation it best fits. Use each word once.

1. using the Internet
   _____

2. shouting of sports fans
   _____

3. studying for a test
   _____

4. taking a trip around the world
   _____

5. destroying the ozone layer
   _____

6. cheering someone on in a race
   _____

7. waiting for a big date
   _____

8. wearing all black and walking at night
   _____

9. cleaning the house together
   _____

10. knowing someone is behind you
    _____

Vocabulary Words

| anticipate | avid | trend | endanger | stimulate |
| global | cooperate | benefit | awareness | depletion |

CHAPTER 17   THE ENVIRONMENT

Finish the story with the words below. Use each word once.

Carol wanted to help the environment, so she decided to start with her neighborhood. She knew the first step was _____. People had to be told there was a problem and be shown how they could help. Carol decided that to _____ interest in recycling and other environmental issues she would have an Environmental Fair with food, games, and information booths at the neighborhood park. She knew there were some _____ environmentalists in her neighborhood like Edward Ruiz. Edward recycled everything, drove an electric car, and joined protests to save _____ animals. Carol went to Edwards's house to discuss the Fair.

"What do you think I should make the priority at the Fair? What is our number-one problem?"

"Carol, have you _____ all the problems you will have putting on this event?"

"I know it won't be easy, but since it will _____ the Earth, I am willing to work hard. I also know there are people who will _____ with me in organizing this event—like you."

"Okay, Carol, you have my participation. Let's think _____ and then narrow down our ideas to the neighborhood. We can have a display on the _____ of resources worldwide and then show our neighbors how they can help to save those resources."

"One of the _____ that I want to support is recycling, with bins for paper, plastic, and cans all over the park. Maybe the bins can even stay after the Fair."

"That's a great idea. I have some thoughts on the food we can offer and fun environmental games. Let's sit down and start planning. I am proud of you, Carol, for taking this on!"

Vocabulary Words				
benefit	avid	awareness	depletion	endangered
trends	cooperate	stimulate	globally	anticipated

CHAPTER 17   THE ENVIRONMENT

CHAPTER 18

Word Parts II

Look for words with these **prefixes**, **roots**, and/or **suffixes** as you work through this book. You may have already seen some of them, and you will see others in later chapters. Learning basic word parts can help you figure out what unfamiliar words mean.

prefix: a word part that is added to the beginning of a word and changes the meaning of the root
root: a word's basic part with its essential meaning
suffix: a word part that is added to the end of a word and signifies its part of speech

WORD PART	MEANING	EXAMPLES AND DEFINITIONS
Prefixes		
mal-	bad, wrong	*malicious:* full of malice or wanting to do wrong *malfunction:* working badly
un-	not	*uncharted:* not charted or mapped *unwanted:* not wanted or desired
in-, im-, il-, ir-	in, into, on	*intention:* plan to do *impress:* have an impact on
in-, im-, il-, ir-	not	*invincible:* not able to be hurt *immovable:* not able to move; set
pro-	for, a lot	*productive:* making a lot; constructive *provide:* to foresee; to prepare
Roots		
-vis-, -vid-	see	*evident:* clearly seen *television:* a device for viewing images
-que-, -quir-	to seek	*acquire:* to get something *request:* to seek permission
-spect-	look at	*inspection:* the act of looking into something *spectator:* someone who looks at something
-gen-	birth, creation	*generate:* to create something *generous:* willing to give or share
-scrib-, -script-	write	*manuscript:* a written document *scribble:* to write quickly
Suffixes		
-ate, -ize	to make	*anticipate:* to wait for; to look forward to *empathize:* to be understanding of
-able, -ible	capable of	*admirable:* capable of admiring or approving *possible:* capable of being done

WORD PART	MEANING	EXAMPLES AND DEFINITIONS
Suffixes (continued)		
-ive	performing an action	*offensive:* the action of offending or causing anger *decorative:* the action of decorating or looking nice
-ness	state of being	*awareness:* the state of being aware or knowing *sadness:* the state of being sad or unhappy
-ly	in this manner	*nobly:* done in a noble manner or with superiority *carefully:* done in a careful manner, paying attention

Self-Tests

1 Read the definition, and supply the missing word. Use each word once. The meaning of the word part is underlined to help you make the connection. Refer to the Words Parts list (pages 78 and 79) if you need help.

1. working <u>a lot</u> _____
2. in a noble <u>manner</u> _____
3. <u>to look into</u> something _____
4. <u>to create</u> something _____
5. <u>to make</u> part of memory _____
6. <u>not</u> capable of being hurt _____
7. plainly <u>seen</u> _____
8. <u>not</u> logical _____
9. <u>capable of being</u> done _____
10. a <u>written</u> document _____

Vocabulary Words
productive
manuscript
doable
memorize
nobly
inspect
illogical
evident
generate
invincible

2 Finish the sentences with the meaning for each word part. Use each meaning once. The word part is underlined to help you make the connection.

1. Because the <u>in</u>visible man was impossible to _____, he could overhear a lot of gossip about h<u>im</u>self.

2. My <u>in</u>tention was to become a lawyer. I wanted to go _____ law to help others.

3. The plan was <u>ir</u>regular because we usually meet at one o'clock and _____ at two.

CHAPTER 18 WORD PARTS II 79

4. It is impossible for me to attend the meeting at 6 a.m.; I am not _____ getting up that early.

5. When something malfunctions, it goes _____.

6. The _____ sad is called sadness.

7. Her generous nature led to the _____ of the fund to help students buy books.

8. He scribbled the note on the back of an envelope. He would later _____ it on a piece of paper.

9. I am going to request tomorrow off from work. When I go _____ my boss's approval, I will tell him how important it is that I go skiing.

10. The decorative hanging is _____ of making the room more cheerful.

Vocabulary Words				
see	to seek	creation	write	capable of
bad	not	into	state of being	performing an action

3. Finish the story using the word parts below. Use each word part once. Your knowledge of word parts, as well as the context clues, will help you create the correct words. If you do not understand the meaning of a word you have made, check your dictionary for the definition or to see if the word exists.

The Search

Tony and Edie were looking for an _____ expensive apartment to rent. Neither of them had jobs that _____ vided much money. They in _____ red about availability at one place and were told to come see it. The place was _____ acular. The complex had a pool, a recreation area, and a laundry room. The bedrooms were so large they could easily accommod _____ four people. However, they were _____ able to work it into their budgets.

They thought the chance of finding a two-bedroom apartment within their price range was _____ possible.

Then a friend called and said she had just seen an ad on tele_____ion for apartments. The apartments were supposed to be afford_____. They called the number she gave them, and in two days they found the perfect place. Their happi_____ was now complete.

Vocabulary Words

| in | vis | able | ate | pro |
| qui | spect | un | im | ness |

4. Pick the best definition for the underlined word. Use your knowledge of word parts to help you determine the definition.

1. He is a <u>prolific</u> writer; he has written fifty novels this year.
    a. producing a lot   b. not important   c. done badly

2. The <u>vista</u> of the lake from the path among the elms looked inviting.
    a. plan   b. view   c. taste

3. The <u>genesis</u> of the idea for Sarah's surprise party came from Sarah herself.
    a. writing something   b. do something wrong   c. the creation of something

4. It is <u>probable</u> that I will be late to the meeting because I am coming from across town, and the traffic is bad at noon.
    a. able to see   b. capable of being true   c. for a long time

5. The babysitter's actions were <u>irresponsible</u>—how could she leave a baby alone in a bathtub?
    a. a lot of trust   b. not trustworthy   c. state of being trusted

6. After some <u>introspection</u> Gloria knew which job would be the best for her.
    a. make a quick decision   b. stay away from plans   c. look into one's feelings

7. There was an <u>influx</u> of students to the college when the school began to offer more literature courses; students had been wanting to read more.
    a. a going out   b. a steady amount   c. a coming in

8. When I tried to find my friend to get the money he owed me, he was very <u>elusive</u>.
    a. hard to find   b. one who is hard to find   c. finding again

9. My latest <u>conquest</u> was Mount Whitney. Now I have climbed every peak in the state.
    a. give up   b. move away   c. overcome

10. I should not always <u>criticize</u> my brother; sometimes I need to say something nice.
    a. to write slowly   b. to make a judgment   c. to give birth

CHAPTER 19

Volunteering

So, you want to be a volunteer?

1 Tell me why you think you'd like to work with the **elderly**.

2 I will be elderly someday, so I'd like to **encourage** these senior citizens to have some fun. I hope there will be someone around to **empower** me when I'm in their situation.

3 Many of our patients are **disabled** by the conditions **associated** with old age, such as arthritis, diabetes, and heart conditions. Many of our patients have lost the ability to move around easily, and they are in pain, so sometimes they don't show their **appreciation** for what our volunteers do in quite the way we wish they would. Are you able to make a **commitment** to working with people who have these difficult **afflictions**?

4 Oh yes, my cousin had polio as a child and is in a wheelchair, so I have some experience with that kind of thing. I am willing to **devote** my time to help in any way I can.

5 Well, it seems as though you have a **realistic** view of what we do here. We look forward to having you around.

Predicting

Circle the definition that seems to best fit each vocabulary word. If you have difficulty, return to the reading on page 82, and underline any context clues you find. These clues can help you guess the word's meaning. When you have made your predictions, check your answers against the Word List below. Use the boxes to checkmark those words whose definitions you missed—these are the words you'll want to study closely.

NOTE: You may want to cover the Word List below with a piece of paper so you don't accidentally see the definitions as you do the Predicting exercise.

❏ 1. **elderly** (bubble 1)
   a. retired teachers
   b. old people
   c. old food

❏ 2. **encourage** (bubble 2)
   a. to give hope
   b. to give diapers
   c. to give your time

❏ 3. **empower** (bubble 2)
   a. to give packages
   b. to give water
   c. to give power

❏ 4. **disabled** (bubble 3)
   a. without any money
   b. without food
   c. without certain abilities

❏ 5. **associated** (bubble 3)
   a. connected with
   b. helping with
   c. playing the drums

❏ 6. **appreciation** (bubble 3)
   a. a type of rain
   b. thanks
   c. noise

❏ 7. **commitment** (bubble 3)
   a. an all-girl band
   b. a promise
   c. something like mustard or mayonnaise

❏ 8. **afflictions** (bubble 3)
   a. things causing pain
   b. things smelling bad
   c. positive statements

❏ 9. **devote** (bubble 4)
   a. to give money
   b. to eat liver
   c. to dedicate

❏ 10. **realistic** (bubble 5)
   a. based on facts
   b. based on the future
   c. based on opinion

Word List

affliction [ə flik′ shən]	n.	something that causes pain or distress
appreciation [ə prē′ shē ā′ shən]	n.	feelings of thanks and gratefulness
associated [ə sō′ sē ā təd, ə sō′ shē ā təd]	adj.	to have a connection or relationship with
commitment [kə mit′ mənt]	n.	a duty or promise to do something
devote [dē vōt′]	v.	to dedicate oneself to something; to promise
devoted [dē vōt′ əd]	adj.	dedicated
disabled [dis a′ bəld]	adj.	without certain abilities
elderly [el′ dûr lē]	n.	old people
empower [em pou′ ûr]	v.	to give power to
encourage [en kûr′ ij]	v.	to give hope and confidence to someone
realistic [rē′ ə lis′ tik]	adj.	based on facts

Interactive Exercise

Think about these questions before you answer.

1. Whom do you know who is elderly? _____

2. Whom have you encouraged, or who has encouraged you? _____

3. Name someone who needs to be empowered. _____

4. Do you know someone who has a disability? _____

5. Name three pairs of things that are associated (EXAMPLE: love and marriage).

   _____ and _____   _____ and _____   _____ and _____

6. What is your favorite way to show your appreciation? _____

7. To whom or what have you made a commitment? _____

8. What is the worst affliction you can imagine? _____

9. To what or whom would you be willing to devote your time and money, and why?

   _____

10. Has anyone ever told you that you have a realistic view of something? _____

    How about an unrealistic view? _____

    What was it? _____

Self-Tests

1 Match the quotes with the words they suggest.

Vocabulary Words

| affliction | devote | empower | appreciation | disabled |
| encourage | associated | elderly | realistic | commitment |

_____ 1. "You're eligible for the Senior Citizen's Special!"

_____ 2. "Yes, I'd like to have a family, but I'm not ready to get married."

_____ 3. "Wow! You do that so well that you should become a professional."

84   CHAPTER 19   VOLUNTEERING

_____ 4. "Ice cream and cake just go together. I never think of one without the other."

_____ 5. "I know you can beat that other tennis player!"

_____ 6. "I have given 20 percent of my paycheck and all of my free time to that park project for children."

_____ 7. "You must be reasonable! Not all people are interested in giving ten hours per week to the homeless shelter!"

_____ 8. "Let's all clap our hands in a big round of applause for him!"

_____ 9. "You must get your mind off the red rash on your face; it's only temporary."

_____ 10. "I can't drive the car because it has a flat tire."

▶ 2 Use the vocabulary words to complete these analogies. For instructions on how to complete analogies, see page 135.

1. a drug user : waste ::
   a nun : _____

2. give : take ::
   _____ : discourage

3. honor : Most Valuable Player Award ::
   _____ : cancer

4. young : infant ::
   old: _____

5. black : white ::
   _____ : idealistic

6. similar : alike ::
   connected: _____

7. agreement : contract ::
   promise : _____

8. gasoline : fuel ::
   praise : _____

9. disgust : frowns ::
   _____ : smiles

10. ship : stranded ::
    car : _____

Vocabulary Words

| affliction | devote | empower | appreciation | disabled |
| encourage | associated | elderly | realistic | commitment |

CHAPTER 19 VOLUNTEERING

CHAPTER 20

Complaints

Letter from an **Irate** Customer

M. West
875 Lasso Lane
Del Moro, CA 93000

DM Medical Laboratories
500 Imperial Ave.
Del Moro, CA 93001

Dear DM Medical Laboratories:

I am writing to **clarify** a billing error that your office has made with my account. On August 1, I received a statement from you informing me that my account is more than ninety days **overdue** and that it will soon be turned over to a collection agency. You also stated that this action would cause my credit rating to be **jeopardized**. Your statement is completely incorrect and highly **offensive**.

On April 28 my daughter visited Dr. Bruce Jacobson, an allergy specialist here in Del Moro. He ordered x-rays and blood tests, which were done the same day at your office on Imperial Avenue. I did not receive a bill for these services until July 1, more than two months later. The bill was $310. However, I noticed that you had **neglected** to contact our insurance company, American General, which covers 80% of our medical expenses. I immediately called American General, and I was told that they had not received a **claim** from you for these services. Then I called your business office and spoke with a woman named Wanda. She said that she would contact our insurance company and that I did not need to make a payment until the insurance company had paid. I **assumed** that this matter was **resolved**. Now I have received this second statement from you, demanding full payment of the $310 and **threatening** to take us to a collection agency. I have paid the 20% and my insurance will pay for the rest.

Dr. Jacobson has been our doctor for ten years, and I have spoken to him about the poor service that I have received. I have also reported your office to the Better Business Bureau. It is a shame that customers must suffer when a business is careless.

Sincerely,

Maureen West

Maureen West

Predicting

Circle the definition that seems to best fit each vocabulary word. If you have difficulty, return to the reading on page 86, and underline any context clues you find. These clues can help you guess the word's meaning. When you have made your predictions, check your answers against the Word List below. Use the boxes to checkmark those words whose definitions you missed—these are the words you'll want to study closely.

NOTE: You may want to cover the Word List below with a piece of paper so you don't accidentally see the definitions as you do the Predicting exercise.

❑ 1. **irate** (line 1)
   a. patient
   b. sad
   c. angry

❑ 2. **clarify** (line 9)
   a. to explain
   b. to say
   c. to terrify

❑ 3. **overdue** (line 11)
   a. early
   b. absent
   c. late

❑ 4. **jeopardize** (line 11)
   a. to be on television
   b. to treat unfairly
   c. to risk

❑ 5. **offensive** (line 12)
   a. evident
   b. insulting
   c. untrue

❑ 6. **neglect** (line 17)
   a. to erase
   b. to fail to do
   c. embarrass

❑ 7. **claim** (line 20)
   a. request for payment
   b. intention
   c. criminal report

❑ 8. **assume** (line 22)
   a. to take advantage of
   b. to believe
   c. to assign

❑ 9. **resolve** (line 23)
   a. to refuse
   b. to relocate
   c. to solve

❑ 10. **threaten** (line 24)
   a. to hide
   b. to express intent to harm
   c. to strike

Word List

assume [ə sōōm′]	v.	to suppose, to believe
claim [klām]	n. v.	request to declare to be true
clarify [klâr′ ə fī]	v.	to make clear; to explain
irate [ī rāt′]	adj.	very angry; furious
jeopardize [jep′ ûr dīz]	v.	to risk
neglect [ni glekt′]	v.	to fail to pay attention to; to overlook
offensive [ô fen′ siv, ə fen′ siv]	adj.	insulting
overdue [ō′ vûr dōō′]	adj.	past due; tardy
resolve [rē zôlv′]	v.	to find a solution to; to solve
threaten [thret′ ən]	v.	to put in danger

Interactive Exercise

GET ANGRY IN WRITING

Think of a time when you felt **irate** because you were treated rudely or were overcharged by a business. Write a letter to the company, explaining your side. Use at least seven vocabulary words.

Dear _____ :

Self-Tests

1. Fill in the blank with the vocabulary word that you associate with each of the following sentences:

1. I suppose she's telling the truth. _____
2. We want to find some kind of solution. _____
3. That man over there looks so angry. _____
4. Please explain this. _____
5. Uh-oh. I forgot to take that book back to the library. Now it's late. _____
6. He said if I don't pay him back, he'll beat me up. _____
7. After the accident, I had to fill out a lot of paperwork for my insurance company. _____
8. She said some ugly things that really hurt me. _____
9. Justin doesn't pay any attention to his little brother. _____
10. Don't risk your life by not wearing a seatbelt! _____

Vocabulary Words
resolve
irate
claim
offensive
jeopardize
clarify
assume
neglect
threaten
overdue

2. Fill in the blank with one of the vocabulary words from the bottom of the page.

I received a _____ phone call last night from a collection agency. It was horrible. A rude woman from ABC Collections in Del Moro said that several payments on my Ford Explorer were _____. She _____ to give me any specific information, just that I had _____ my credit by not paying my bills. The problem is that I do not even own a Ford Explorer! I tried to _____ this and explain myself, but she didn't give me a chance to respond. I'm so _____ about this that I could scream! I had to listen to this rude woman with her _____ tone of voice. I have absolutely no idea how or why this has happened to me—I just want to _____ this as soon as possible. Maybe they'll realize they've made a mistake, but I can't _____ anything. I'm going to call an attorney and file a _____ against ABC Collections. These things shouldn't happen!

Vocabulary Words

| resolve | assume | jeopardized | offensive | clarify |
| claim | threatening | overdue | neglected | irate |

CHAPTER 20 COMPLAINTS 89

CHAPTER 21

Review: Focus on Chapters 11–20

For instructions, see page 91.

1. _____

2. _____

3. _____

4. _____

5. _____

6. _____

7. _____

8. _____

9. _____

10. _____

11. _____

12. _____

13. _____

14. _____

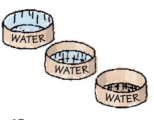
15. _____

The following activities give you a chance to interact some more with the vocabulary words you've been learning. By looking at art, acting, writing, taking tests, and doing a crossword puzzle, you will see which words you know well and which you still need to work with.

Art

Match each picture on page 90 to one of the following vocabulary words. Use each word once.

Vocabulary Words

tenderness	hieroglyphics	gossip	depletion	reservation
lament	ballot	souvenir	elderly	excursion
disabled	queue	epitaph	threatening	nobly

Drama

Charades: You will be given one of the following words to act out in class. Think about how this word can be demonstrated without speaking. The other people in class will try to guess what word you are showing.

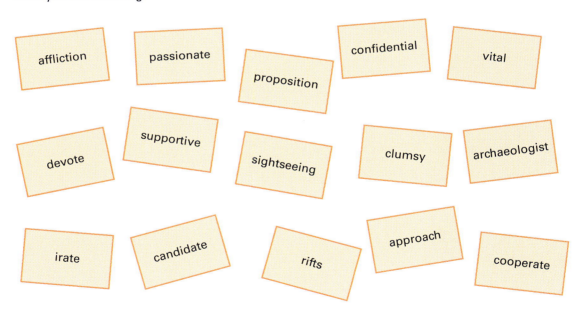

CHAPTER 21 REVIEW

Writing

Answer the following questions to further test your understanding of the vocabulary words:

1. What trends do you think have been silly? _____
   _____

2. How can you show your commitment to school? _____
   _____

3. What is a realistic goal you should set for yourself? _____
   _____

4. Whom would you share an intimate secret with? Why? _____
   _____

5. What is one of the most offensive smells to you? _____

6. What can people do to overcome gullibility? _____
   _____

7. What areas are still uncharted in this world? _____

8. When should you be accurate? _____

9. How much time do you budget each week for homework? For time with friends?
   _____

10. Who is someone you can empathize with? _____

11. When were you willing to compromise? _____
    _____

12. What sport are you avid about? Or whom do you know who is an avid sports fan?
    _____

13. What events would it be good to establish a timetable for? _____
    _____

14. What have you felt unbridled enthusiasm for? _____
    _____

15. When was the last time you were inconvenienced? _____
    _____

Self-Tests

 Finish the story using the vocabulary words below. There will be five words left over.

The Party

I thought that throwing a party to show my _____ to all my friends for their support when I was ill would be easy: I was wrong. First, I didn't think of the _____ involved in such a project. My original _____ that it would cost about $100 was way too low. It was obvious that I needed to change my _____ plan after a trip to the party store where I spent $105 on decorations, plates, and games. I then _____ that I would make a firm budget. If I was going to be able to _____ with this event, I would need to plan carefully.

The night of the party arrived, and I _____ how nice my house looked. I was _____ about the success of the party when the first guests complimented me about the good food and beautiful decorations. Then something _____ happened, and the mood of the party began to change as more people came. My _____ of the problem was slow, but I came to feel that there was tension in the room. To _____ my feelings, I asked my best friend. She had always been _____ and would tell me the truth. She told me that someone had started a _____ story about me. I was _____ that someone would say mean things about me. How could one of my friends do that? I cautiously tried to find the _____ of the person who was spreading the gossip. His or her cover, however, was _____.

Finally, I stood up on a chair and said, "For the _____ of everyone here, I want to announce that the story about me is not true. My illness and the support of real friends have _____ me to make this statement. I had _____ that everyone here was a friend. _____, I was wrong. To those people who really do care about me, thank you for coming to my party." As the clapping began, I heard the front door open and shut. I never figured out who left, but I enjoyed the rest of the evening with some great friends.

Vocabulary Words

admired
affronted
apparently
appreciation
assumed
awareness
benefit
clumsy
cope
disclosed
empowered
encouraged
estimate
expenses
identity
invincible
loyal
malicious
preliminary
queue
remarkable
resolved
stimulate
uncharted
verify

CHAPTER 21 REVIEW 93

Pick the word that best completes the sentence.

1. I didn't _____ my homework taking so long. Now I don't know if I will finish.
   a. fascination b. anticipate c. clarify d. cooperate

2. Anita _____ her free time to helping children learn to read.
   a. verifies b. copes c. admires d. devotes

3. He showed his _____ when he bought low and sold high in the stock market.
   a. passionate b. proposition c. shrewdness d. tenderness

4. I was shocked when Elizabeth _____ her secret that she was from outer space.
   a. disclosed b. resolved c. assumed d. associated

5. Karl was _____ that the store was closed; he really wanted a bag of potato chips.
   a. affliction b. irate c. neglect d. clumsy

6. I have to make sure my math is _____ when I do my taxes. I don't want a fine.
   a. estimate b. overdue c. authentic d. accurate

7. Rosanne, it is _____ that you be on time for the big meeting—we can't lose this account.
   a. avid b. threatening c. vital d. offensive

8. The painting was so _____ I thought it was a photograph.
   a. invincible b. realistic c. global d. disabled

9. Brian accepted his blue ribbon at the pie baking contest _____; he acted as if he had been awarded the Nobel Peace Prize.
   a. elderly b. gullibility c. rifts d. nobly

10. Christen _____ ever taking the trip. It was one disaster after another.
    a. lamented b. gossiped c. stimulated d. cooperated

Crossword Puzzle

Use the following words to complete the crossword puzzle. You will use each word once.

Vocabulary Words

absentee
advice
anticipate
associated
attendants
authenticity
bereavement
chronological
claim
clarify
disclose
endangered
fascination
global
jeopardize
manuscript
neglect
overdue
poll
prognosis
proxy
reveal
shrewdness
stimulate
sympathy

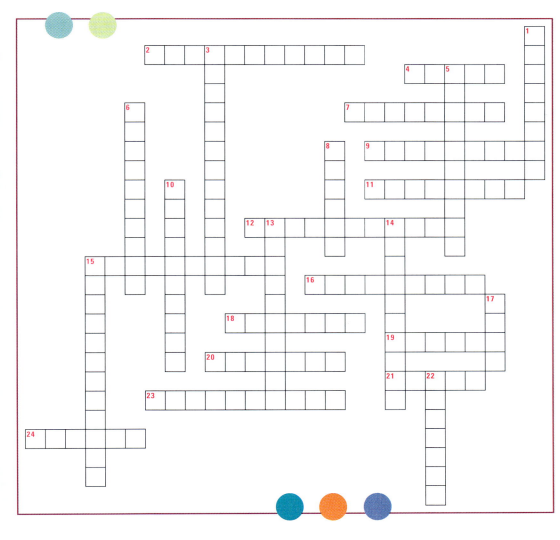

Across

2. an extreme interest in
4. I say it is true.
7. a person who is not there
9. what the doctor gives
11. the kind of card one would send to a widow
12. sadness
15. related to
16. to excite
18. He didn't do his homework.
19. to show
20. I needed to _____ my points, so people would understand my side.
21. to take someone's place
23. Being dishonest with a friend could do this to the friendship.
24. This can be good or bad.

Down

1. to tell the truth about
3. time order
5. parking and flight are two types
6. cleverness
8. the whole world
10. to look forward to
13. panda bears are this
14. a written document
15. Check the _____ of an antique before you buy it.
17. to ask people the same question
22. It's about time!

CHAPTER 21 REVIEW 95

CHAPTER 22

Television

Monday Night Channel Surfing

1 "Zebra almost invariably remain with the herd, as opposed to wandering off alone or in small family groups. This annual crossing of the river during their migration from summer to winter grazing areas is attended by crocodile, as well as the wildebeeste." (The **narrator's** deep voice is heard above the sights and sounds of zebras and crocodiles splashing in the river.) "This habit of remaining in the herd is a type of defense against enemies."

click

2 I'm not in the mood to watch a **documentary**.

3 "I always eat Wacky Wonder Breakfast Toast! It's the one the kids all love to eat because it has so many pretty colors…AND it's good for them too. It's fortified with 80 vitamins and minerals."

click

4 Stupid **commercial**!

5 "Our **nightly** weather **forecast** is next! Stay tuned to see how much rain we're expecting for tomorrow's parade!"

click

6 Oh, GREAT, this guy can't predict what day of the week tomorrow will be, let alone the weather. I feel like watching a nice talk show, one with an intelligent **host**.

7 "We **interrupt** this **broadcast** to inform our viewers of the possibility of severe storms over the next few hours. Use caution due to the possibility of lightning and strong winds. Driving should be avoided. We will keep you informed of any new developments. Stay tuned for our nightly **newscast**. We return to the program in progress."

8 Where'd my show go? That darn storm has ruined the **reception**!

Predicting

Circle the definition that seems to best fit each vocabulary word. If you have difficulty, return to the reading on page 96, and underline any context clues you find. These clues can help you guess the word's meaning. When you have made your predictions, check your answers against the Word List below. Use the boxes to checkmark those words whose definitions you missed—these are the words you'll want to study closely.

NOTE: You may want to cover the Word List below with a piece of paper so you don't accidentally see the definitions as you do the Predicting exercise.

☐ 1. **narrator** (bubble 1)
   a. bank teller
   b. storyteller
   c. tour bus driver

☐ 2. **documentary** (bubble 2)
   a. a factual drama
   b. a funny drama
   c. a love story

☐ 3. **commercial** (bubble 4)
   a. a joke
   b. a political party
   c. an advertisement on TV or radio

☐ 4. **nightly** (bubble 5)
   a. happens every night
   b. happens when you least expect it
   c. late

☐ 5. **forecast** (bubble 5)
   a. what is believed will happen
   b. a type of utensil
   c. a balloon

☐ 6. **host** (bubble 6)
   a. a person receiving guests
   b. a god
   c. a big game animal

☐ 7. **interrupt** (bubble 7)
   a. to break a dish
   b. to break the flow of
   c. to break dance

☐ 8. **broadcast** (bubble 7)
   a. a large person
   b. program on TV or radio
   c. a movement of fishing

☐ 9. **newscast** (bubble 7)
   a. a net for fishing
   b. a newspaper
   c. a news report on TV or radio

☐ 10. **reception** (bubble 8)
   a. fun
   b. repeat
   c. electronic signal

Word List

broadcast [brôd′ kast′]	n.	a program sent out over radio or TV
	v.	1. the act of sending out a signal (electronic) 2. to make generally known
commercial [kə mûr′ shəl]	n.	broadcast advertisement
documentary [dok′ yōō men′ tə rē]	n.	factual dramatized report
forecast [fôr′ kast′]	n.	statement that predicts something
	v.	the act of telling in advance what is going to happen
host [hōst]	n.	person who receives another as his or her guest
	v.	to act as a host
interrupt [in′ tə rupt′]	v.	to break the continuity or flow of something
narrator [nâr′ āt ûr]	n.	the person who tells a story
newscast [nōōz′ kast′]	n.	a broadcast news report
nightly [nīt′ lē]	adv.	happening every night
reception [rē sep′ shən]	n.	the receiving of electronic signals

Interactive Exercise

For each topic or category, give five examples.

Names of Narrators or Types of Programs with Narrators:

1. _____
2. _____
3. _____
4. _____
5. _____

Names or Types of Nightly Broadcasts:

1. _____
2. _____
3. _____
4. _____
5. _____

Names of Talk Show Hosts:

1. _____
2. _____
3. _____
4. _____
5. _____

Subjects for Documentaries:

1. _____
2. _____
3. _____
4. _____
5. _____

Activities That Could Be Interrupted:

1. _____
2. _____
3. _____
4. _____
5. _____

Items Advertised on TV Commercials:

1. _____
2. _____
3. _____
4. _____
5. _____

Self-Tests

1 Fill in the blanks using the vocabulary words on page 99.

I hate _____ on TV. They waste my time by talking about things I don't want to buy. I also hate it when the _____ is poor; it makes it difficult to watch my favorite programs. My favorite _____ come on every evening. My favorite _____ is *World News Tonight with Peter Jennings.*

_____, Peter Jennings updates me on what has happened in the world during the day. Of course, I enjoy making fun of the weather _____, which are almost never correct for my area of the country. It's difficult to predict the weather here because we have so many local weather conditions that are difficult to see on the large maps used by the weather service. So, our local TV programs are often _____ for weather bulletins.

Late last night I fell asleep watching a talk show. It was a wild one with the _____ fighting with the guests. I was so tired that it might as well have been a fact-filled, boring _____. The trouble with documentaries late at night is that they usually have soft-spoken _____, who put me to sleep instantly.

Vocabulary Words

| broadcasts | host | newscast | commercials | interrupted |
| nightly | documentary | narrators | reception | forecasts |

2. Use each of the vocabulary words to complete these analogies. For instructions on how to complete analogies, see page 135.

1. school : textbook ::
   TV : _____

2. bedtime : storyteller ::
   book, radio, or TV: _____

3. magazine : advertisement ::
   radio : _____

4. sun : daily ::
   moon : _____

5. reading: newspaper ::
   TV : _____

6. dirty : windshield ::
   poor : _____

7. news: report ::
   weather : _____

8. school : teacher ::
   party : _____

9. dinner : belch ::
   conversation : _____

10. bell : rings ::
    TV station : _____

Vocabulary Words

broadcasts
host
newscast
commercial
interrupt
nightly
documentary
narrator
reception
forecast

CHAPTER 23

Books

REVIEWS
BOOK REVIEW DIGEST

The work of **fiction** I'm reviewing today is less interesting than the average dictionary! It's been **panned** by all the other **critics**, and I can see no reason not to join them.

The characters are **stereotypes** rather than having any **resemblance** to any real people, at least on this planet.

The book's length is another point of **contention**. Why does this author think that adding pages to his book adds to the importance of his book as literature? His **prose** is far too **monotonous** for me to be glad to read even one more sentence. The last three chapters are **superfluous**, not necessary at all. This author has made reading a **burden** rather than the usual pleasure I find it to be. Any reader who completes this tome deserves a free trip, all expenses paid, to Hawaii compliments of the author.

Predicting

Circle the definition that seems to best fit each vocabulary word. If you have difficulty, return to the reading on page 100, and underline any context clues you find. These clues can help you guess the word's meaning. When you have made your predictions, check your answers against the Word List below. Use the boxes to checkmark those words whose definitions you missed—these are the words you'll want to study closely.

NOTE: You may want to cover the Word List below with a piece of paper so you don't accidentally see the definitions as you do the Predicting exercise.

❏ 1. **fiction** (line 1)
   a. not true
   b. not useful
   c. not fun

❏ 2. **panned** (line 3)
   a. put into a pan on the stove
   b. criticized
   c. written

❏ 3. **critic** (line 3)
   a. fruit
   b. a person who gives opinions
   c. a live show with lions

❏ 4. **stereotype** (line 5)
   a. a person representing a group, but having no individual characteristics
   b. a cassette tape
   c. a person who stands out as an individual

❏ 5. **resemblance** (line 6)
   a. difference
   b. assembly
   c. similarity

❏ 6. **contention** (line 8)
   a. done on purpose
   b. argument
   c. invention

❏ 7. **prose** (line 11)
   a. poetry
   b. music
   c. not poetry

❏ 8. **monotonous** (line 11)
   a. boring
   b. really big
   c. having to do with sheep

❏ 9. **superfluous** (line 13)
   a. fast
   b. easy
   c. too much

❏ 10. **burden** (line 15)
   a. a cold room
   b. a difficult job
   c. a brand of cheese

Word List

burden [bûr′ dən]	n. a difficult job, task, or load to carry	**panned** [pand]	v. badly criticized
contention [kən ten′ shən]	n. an argument	**prose** [prōz]	n. language that is not poetry
critic [krit′ ik]	n. a person whose job is to share his or her opinions, good or bad, about books, movies, art, music, etc.	**resemblance** [rē zem′ bləns]	n. similarity to another person, place, or thing
fiction [fik′ shən]	n. a made-up or invented story; not factual	**stereotype** [stâr′ ē ō tīp′]	n. a standardized idea or character with no individual features; a set of characteristics used to classify people
monotonous [mə not′ ən əs]	adj. having no variety; boring	**superfluous** [soo pûr′ floo əs]	adj. more than is needed

Interactive Exercise

Answer the following questions:

1. Name a burden that you would like to give away. _____

   What would you exchange for it? _____

2. Name something that has been a point of contention between you and a friend.
   _____

3. When have you been a critic? _____

4. What is your favorite work of fiction? _____

5. Name something that you find monotonous. _____

6. Name a movie that was panned by the critics (or your family). _____

7. What is your favorite piece of prose? _____

8. Is there a resemblance between you and any well-known personality? _____

   Who? _____ What is the resemblance? _____

9. Name a common stereotype. _____
   _____

10. Think of a celebration you have attended. What items were superfluous?
    _____

Self-Tests

> **1** Match the vocabulary words on page 103 to the sentences they best fit.

_____ 1. They always comment about the sets in a play, as well as the action and characters.

_____ 2. All the sentences were the same length, and even the words all had about five to ten letters. And all the time I was reading, I was wishing I'd chosen another article to read.

_____ 3. She wanted to watch *Mission Impossible,* but he wanted to watch the football game. They didn't seem happy for several days after that.

_____ 4. All of the entertainment columns I read seemed to agree that the movie was not worth wasting time or money for—very bad indeed!

_____ 5. My family watched seven films over the weekend. Two would have been enough for me.

_____ 6. Our English professor asked us to read an entire novel and write three essays in the past two weeks.

_____ 7. The movies *The Bishop's Wife,* which was made in the forties, and the *Preacher's Wife,* which was made in the nineties, have the same story.

_____ 8. In love stories, the hero always gets the girl.

_____ 9. It rhymes with *rose, nose,* and *toes.*

_____ 10. The story begins with a cowboy who really loves his horse and hates the interfering mother of his beautiful wife who fell in love with the handsome doctor who treated her when she fell off the jealous horse.

Vocabulary Words

| burden | critics | monotonous | prose | stereotypes |
| contention | fiction | panned | resemblance | superfluous |

2 Use the vocabulary words to complete these analogies. For instructions on how to complete analogies, see page 135.

1. true : false ::
   fact : _____

2. classical : rock ::
   poetry : _____

3. attorney : judge ::
   writer : _____

4. art : artifact ::
   resemble : _____

5. war : peace ::
   harmony : _____

6. give : take ::
   easy : _____

7. eagle : bird of prey ::
   dumb blonde: _____

8. black : white ::
   praised : _____

9. small : skimpy ::
   large : _____

10. boring : stimulating ::
    exciting : _____

Vocabulary Words

| burden | monotonous | resemblance | contention | panned |
| stereotypes | critic | prose | superfluous | fiction |

CHAPTER 23   BOOKS

CHAPTER 24

Movies

Movie Favorites

Dear Joe,

Did you see they came out with another one of those 100 Greatest Movies Ever list? The magazines give those lists so much **hype** and then they run a TV special about the list. I love movies, but there is too much publicity for these things, especially when the lists
5 have been so lame. I don't want to argue with this latest one too much, but I would never put Rocky on my top 100. Come on. The plot was so **contrived**. I knew he was going to win.

As movie **buffs**, we need to **generate** our own list. We also need some other **categories**. How about the ten most **villainous** characters
10 ever? Definitely on my list is the Wicked Witch of the West in The Wonderful Wizard of Oz. She's so mean! I can already predict who you will have on your list—Darth Vader. If you can pick anything from Star Wars, you will. What about the biggest **blunders** in movie history? Remaking Godzilla certainly **qualifies**. That movie was awful.
15 What is your favorite opening **sequence** for a movie? One of mine is from High Noon. I love watching the horses run and wondering what's going to happen. And, of course, the music is great. What other areas should we include in our **superlative** movie lists?

Write me back soon.
20 Your friend,
Roger

Predicting

Circle the definition that seems to best fit each vocabulary word. If you have difficulty, return to the reading on page 104, and underline any context clues you find. These clues can help you guess the word's meaning. When you have made your predictions, check your answers against the Word List below. Use the boxes to checkmark those words whose definitions you missed—these are the words you'll want to study closely.

NOTE: You may want to cover the Word List below with a piece of paper so you don't accidentally see the definitions as you do the Predicting exercise.

❏ 1. **hype** (line 4)
   a. a walk
   b. excess promotion
   c. look for something

❏ 2. **contrived** (line 8)
   a. real
   b. great
   c. fake

❏ 3. **buff** (line 9)
   a. empty
   b. an admirer
   c. a lazy person

❏ 4. **generate** (line 9)
   a. to start up
   b. to finish
   c. to file

❏ 5. **category** (line 10)
   a. a group
   b. a scary cat
   c. a small room

❏ 6. **villainous** (line 10)
   a. evil
   b. kind
   c. weak

❏ 7. **blunder** (line 14)
   a. a mistake
   b. opposite of lightning
   c. eye covering

❏ 8. **qualify** (line 15)
   a. to be thrown out
   b. to meet the requirements
   c. to run wild

❏ 9. **sequence** (line 16)
   a. an underwater world
   b. a type of fruit
   c. a logical order

❏ 10. **superlative** (line 19)
   a. a low tone
   b. a hero
   c. an exaggerated expression

Word List

blunder [blun′ dûr]	n.	a mistake	**hype** [hīp]	n. excess promotion
	v.	to make a mistake		
buff [buf]	n.	admirer; follower	**qualify** [kwäl′ ə fī′]	v. to meet the requirements
category [kat′ ə gôr′ ē]	n.	a class, group, or division	**sequence** [sē′ kwəns]	n. arrangement in a logical order
contrived [kən trīvd′]	adj.	lacking spontaneity; artificial; fake	**superlative** [soo pûr′ lə tiv]	n. an exaggerated expression, usually of praise
generate [jen′ ə rāt′]	v.	to start up; to develop	**villainous** [vil′ ə nəs]	adv. evil; very wicked

Interactive Exercise

Generate two responses for each of the following:

Most *Villainous* Characters
1. _____
2. _____

Most *Contrived* Scenes
1. _____
2. _____

Most *Hyped* Movies
1. _____
2. _____

Favorite Opening *Sequence*
1. _____
2. _____

What *Qualifies* You to Judge Movies
1. _____
2. _____

Movies in the Action *Category*
1. _____
2. _____

Often-Used *Superlatives* About Movies
1. _____
2. _____

Types of Movie *Buff* You Are
1. _____
2. _____

Biggest Movie *Blunders*
1. _____
2. _____

Self-Tests

 Circle the correct meaning of each word.

1. hype: ignore   go on about
2. villainous: behave badly   do good
3. blunder: perfect   make a mistake
4. generate: create   finish
5. contrived: fake   true
6. category: a logical group   doesn't fit anywhere
7. qualify: has the skill   hasn't a clue
8. sequence: first this, then this   random
9. buff: excited about   couldn't care less
10. superlative: greatest   nice enough

As you read the following story, write down the word that each scene suggests. Context clues are underlined to help you. Use each word once.

Julie and Diana decide to go to the movies on Saturday night. As they approach the multiplex, finishing their sodas from <u>the James Bond cups</u> they got at the fast food restaurant, they see a <u>huge billboard for the new Bond movie</u>. 1. _____

Julie and Diana, however, aren't going to the Bond film because <u>they love romances</u>. They <u>must see</u> the movie about a woman who finds love while traveling in South America. 2. _____

They sit down just in time for the beginning. <u>From a distance</u> the camera shows a boat slowly sailing down the Amazon at sunset. <u>Then</u> the camera comes in closer to show a blond woman in a white evening dress, boa, and a huge jewel-studded necklace walking toward one of the cabins. <u>Finally</u>, she enters the cabin, and the door closes behind her. 3. _____

A dark-haired woman exits the cabin moments later with <u>a mean look</u> in her eye. She is <u>holding a gun</u> and a large emerald. She quickly puts both of them in a bag. She signals to a small boat close by and disappears in it. Someone yells, <u>"Murder."</u> 4. _____

Sandra Bullet, a private detective, rushes out of her cabin. At the same time, two doors down, Antonio Dashing thrusts open his door. Julie whispers to Diana, "These two certainly belong in the <u>good-looking division</u>." 5. _____

Sandra and Antonio meet at the door of the cabin of the murdered woman. Antonio stares appreciatively at Sandra, but stops her from entering. "I'm with the Secret Service, and I don't want any <u>mistakes</u> made here," he tells her. 6. _____

Sandra explains, "I am a detective. <u>I know what needs to be done</u> and <u>how to do it right</u>." 7. _____

Antonio looks at her and nods, "I'm sure you do. Come, join me in solving this case." Diana whispers to Julie, "This is going to <u>develop</u> into a hot romance." Julie nods. 8. _____

As the movie progresses, Sandra and Antonio work together to find the missing emerald of the Incas and end up falling in love. When the movie is over, Julie gushes, "That was <u>the greatest</u> love story I have ever seen." 9. _____

Diana, on the other hand, says, "Give me a break! It was easy to tell where they were going to find the jewel, how they were going to get it back, and when they were going to go to bed. It was all <u>too fake</u>." 10. _____

Vocabulary Words

| villainous | superlative | category | generate | blunders |
| buffs | contrived | hype | sequence | qualifies |

CHAPTER 24 MOVIES 107

CHAPTER 25

The Workplace

The Annual Review

1 Miss Adams, each year management is required to file a report on every employee. This year, we are considering **downsizing** so we'll use the report to decide which employees to **retain**, and which to release.

2 Yes, Ms. Davis. I do my job very well and I understand that this is just a requirement of the **bureaucracy**, not anything personal, and not anything for me to worry about.

3 Let me begin, Miss Adams. Your **supervisor** says that your secretarial skills (typing, filing, **dictation**) are **adequate**, but that you aren't able to complete things in a **timely** fashion; you're always late!

4 I know that I have trouble meeting all the deadlines. What can I do to improve in this area?

5 Ah, Miss Adams, what a timely question! It's truly **admirable** that you took the **initiative** to ask me what you can do about your problem with time management. Because all your other work is **sufficient** to retain you as an employee, the company will invest in you by sending you to a time-management seminar.

6 Thank you Ms. Davis. I really appreciate my job.

Predicting

Circle the definition that seems to best fit each vocabulary word. If you have difficulty, return to the reading on page 108, and underline any context clues you find. These clues can help you guess the word's meaning. When you have made your predictions, check your answers against the Word List below. Use the boxes to checkmark those words whose definitions you missed—these are the words you'll want to study closely.

NOTE: You may want to cover the Word List below with a piece of paper so you don't accidentally see the definitions as you do the Predicting exercise.

❑ 1. **downsizing** (bubble 1)
   a. riding on an escalator
   b. dieting
   c. making smaller

❑ 2. **retain** (bubble 1)
   a. to keep
   b. to straighten teeth
   c. to learn a new job

❑ 3. **bureaucracy** (bubble 2)
   a. messy drawers
   b. official routine
   c. harmonized voices

❑ 4. **supervisor** (bubble 3)
   a. a person wearing a hat
   b. on the windshield
   c. a person in charge

❑ 5. **dictation** (bubble 3)
   a. a recorded dictionary
   b. a file
   c. words written as they are spoken

❑ 6. **adequate** (bubble 3)
   a. goofy
   b. good enough
   c. carries water

❑ 7. **timely** (bubble 3)
   a. at the perfect time
   b. at any time
   c. all the time

❑ 8. **admirable** (bubble 5)
   a. an officer in the Navy
   b. able to do anything
   c. excellent

❑ 9. **initiative** (bubble 5)
   a. inside
   b. the first step
   c. a ceremony when you join a group

❑ 10. **sufficient** (bubble 5)
   a. enough
   b. thinking only of yourself
   c. really organized

Word List

adequate [ad′ ə kwət] — *adj.* all right, but not wonderful; satisfactory

admirable [ad′ mûr ə bəl] — *adj.* excellent; worthy of praise or admiration

bureaucracy [byoo rok′ rə sē] — *n.* officially required routine that is overdone; organizational structure that is large and often inefficient

dictation [dik tā′ shən] — *n.* language that is written down at the same time that it is heard by the writer

downsizing [doun′ sīz′ ing] — *v.* making a company smaller by changing jobs around and letting some employees go

initiative [i nish′ ə tiv] — *n.* the first step toward beginning something

retain [rē tān′] — *v.* to keep

sufficient [sə fish′ ənt] — *adj.* enough

supervisor [soo′ pûr vī′ zûr] — *n.* a person whose job is to be in charge of workers and their work

timely [tīm′ lē] — *adj.* happening at the perfect time

Interactive Exercise

1. Explain the ways that *downsizing* could affect the lives of employees.
   _____

2. Which items that you own do you want to *retain* for the rest of your life?
   _____

3. Describe some ways in which *bureaucracy* has affected your life.
   _____

4. What sorts of things is a *supervisor* expected to do in his or her job?
   _____

5. Describe the scene of someone taking *dictation*.
   _____

6. Name a skill at which you are just *adequate*. _____

7. Describe a *timely* occurrence in your life. _____

8. Name an *admirable* characteristic of one of your friends or family members.
   _____

9. Explain a situation where you took the *initiative*. _____

10. Name something that you possess in *sufficient* quantity. _____

Self-Tests

> **1** Use the vocabulary words on page 111 to fill in the blanks in the following sentences.

1. He is always on time, looks well groomed, and is polite. He has many of these _____ qualities.

2. When she takes _____, she always turns her head to one side as if she is trying to hear better.

3. I always worry that we will run out of paper clips in the office, but there seems to be a _____ supply right now.

4. My son hasn't done well in the third grade, and I'm afraid that the school wants to _____ him at that level.

5. He's a great guy, but I'm afraid he won't do well in the sales department because people need to be self-starters there, and he has no _____.

CHAPTER 25 THE WORKPLACE

6. I worry about keeping my job because companies all over are _____.

7. I wanted to start my own business, but then I went to the city offices to fill out all of the correct forms and permits. There was so much paperwork and so many places to go to get more paperwork that I was overcome by the _____.

8. She was let go from one company that was downsizing just as another company started up. They offered her a position that paid more money than she made before. It was a very _____ move.

9. My _____ asked me to work overtime this Saturday. I hate to work on Saturdays, but I like the money and don't want to disappoint her.

10. His skills are _____, but he'll never win any awards.

Vocabulary Words

| adequate | downsizing | sufficient | admirable | initiative |
| supervisor | bureaucracy | retain | timely | dictation |

2 Use the clues to fill in the horizontal blanks. Another vocabulary word will appear vertically when the horizontal blanks have been correctly filled in.

10.

1. _ _ _ _ _ _ _ _ _
2. _ _ _ _ _ _ _ _
3. _ _ _ _ _ _ _ _ _ _ _
4. _ _ _ _ _ _
5. _ _ _ _ _ _ _ _
6. _ _ _ _ _ _
7. _ _ _ _ _ _ _ _ _ _
8. _ _ _ _ _ _ _ _ _
9. _ _ _ _ _ _ _ _ _ _

Vocabulary Words

adequate
downsizing
sufficient
admirable
initiative
supervisor
bureaucracy
retain
timely
dictation

CLUES

1. excellent
2. enough
3. "red tape"
4. perfectly scheduled
5. just all right
6. keep
7. the first step
8. the boss
9. making smaller
10. The "hidden word" is: _____

CHAPTER 26

Computers

Lost in (Cyber)space

1 **Char:** This is so embarrassing. My own son can do this, and I'm **clueless**, totally lost. I want to send an e-mail message. I just bought this computer. It's supposed to be for my classes, but he's using it all the time, just
5 **monopolizing** it. I'm going to—

Jimmy: Mom, please stop **muttering** to yourself.

Char: [Okay, I'll swallow my **pride** now.] Jimmy, could you please put your **superior** attitude **aside** for a minute and show me how to send an e-mail?

10 **Jimmy:** Here. This is your in-box. Click on "new message." See how that message form comes out? Now type in Aunt Cammy's e-mail address. See? Put in subject heading. Okay, good. Now you can write your message.

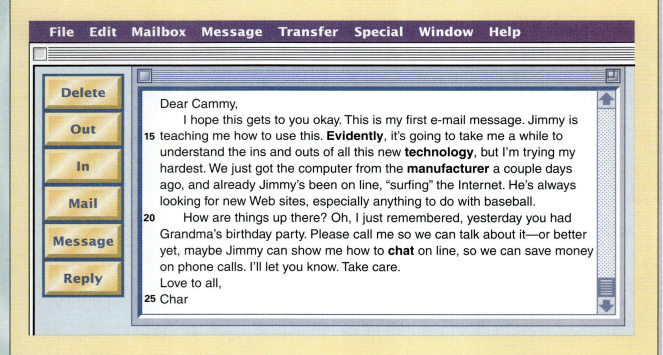

File   Edit   Mailbox   Message   Transfer   Special   Window   Help

Delete / Out / In / Mail / Message / Reply

Dear Cammy,
   I hope this gets to you okay. This is my first e-mail message. Jimmy is
15 teaching me how to use this. **Evidently**, it's going to take me a while to understand the ins and outs of all this new **technology**, but I'm trying my hardest. We just got the computer from the **manufacturer** a couple days ago, and already Jimmy's been on line, "surfing" the Internet. He's always looking for new Web sites, especially anything to do with baseball.
20   How are things up there? Oh, I just remembered, yesterday you had Grandma's birthday party. Please call me so we can talk about it—or better yet, maybe Jimmy can show me how to **chat** on line, so we can save money on phone calls. I'll let you know. Take care.
   Love to all,
25 Char

Predicting

Circle the definition that seems to best fit each vocabulary word. If you have difficulty, return to the reading on page 112, and underline any context clues you find. These clues can help you guess the word's meaning. When you have made your predictions, check your answers against the Word List below. Use the boxes to checkmark those words whose definitions you missed—these are the words you'll want to study closely.

NOTE: You may want to cover the Word List below with a piece of paper so you don't accidentally see the definitions as you do the Predicting exercise.

❏ 1. **clueless** (line 2)
   a. without questions
   b. without understanding
   c. without any glue

❏ 2. **monopolize** (line 5)
   a. to write a letter
   b. to play games
   c. to control

❏ 3. **mutter** (line 6)
   a. to learn
   b. to speak softly and unclearly
   c. to use bad words

❏ 4. **pride** (line 7)
   a. a drink
   b. anger
   c. self-respect

❏ 5. **superior** (line 8)
   a. feeling of being better than others
   b. cold
   c. terrible

❏ 6. **aside** (line 8)
   a. to the side
   b. on your side
   c. inside

❏ 7. **evidently** (line 15)
   a. avidly
   b. increasingly
   c. clearly

❏ 8. **technology** (line 16)
   a. applied science
   b. electricity
   c. high volume

❏ 9. **manufacturer** (line 17)
   a. liar
   b. producer
   c. pitcher

❏ 10. **chat** (line 22)
   a. cast
   b. talk
   c. cheat

Word List

aside [ə sīd']	adv.	1. away 2. to one side
chat [chat]	v. n.	to have a conversation a conversation
clueless [kloo' ləs]	adj.	without understanding; confused
evidently [ev' ə dənt lē, ev' ə dent' lē]	adv.	clearly
evident [ev' ə dənt]	adj.	clear; plain
manufacturer [man' yə fak' chûr ûr]	n.	producer; maker
manufacture [man' yoo fak' chûr]	v.	to produce
monopolize [mə nop' ə līz]	v.	to control; to dominate
mutter [mut' ûr]	v.	to speak softly and unclearly
pride [prīd]	n.	self-respect; confidence
superior [sə pēr' ē ûr]	adj.	1. showing a feeling of being better than others 2. excellent
technology [tek nol' ə jē]	n.	applied science; system design

CHAPTER 26 COMPUTERS

Interactive Exercise

If your school or college has a computer laboratory with access to the Internet, go there alone or with your class. Sign up for an e-mail account through one of the free e-mail providers (if you don't have one already). Your teacher or the lab instructor can give you information on how to do this. After you have an e-mail address, find out the e-mail address of a classmate, another friend, or even one of your teachers. Send a short e-mail message, like the one that Char wrote to Cammy. Use at least five of the vocabulary words. Then, print a copy of your message.

If it is impossible for you to use the Internet, write in the space below:

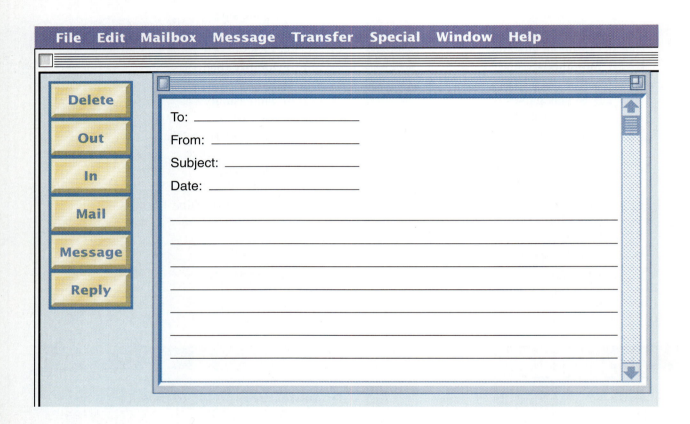

Self-Tests

1 Write a vocabulary word from the list on page 115 next to the sentence that best relates to it.

1. Tony was saying something, but I couldn't hear it. _____

2. She thinks she's smarter than everyone else in the class. _____

3. I was completely lost in math class yesterday. _____

4. Nike® makes sports equipment. _____

CHAPTER 26 COMPUTERS

5. You never get a chance to talk when Donna is here; she takes over the conversation. _____

6. My dad deserves to feel good about our yard because it's the nicest in the neighborhood. _____

7. We had a nice long talk about old times. _____

8. Maybe someday we will clean our houses with the push of a button. _____

9. It's all very clear now. _____

10. Please put the newspaper down or away from your face. _____

Vocabulary Words

evident	aside	monopolize	chat	mutter
superior	clueless	technology	pride	manufacturer

2 Fill in the blank with the vocabulary word that best fits.

1. When we arrived home yesterday, it was _____ that something was wrong.

2. Our burglar alarm has the latest, state-of-the-art _____.

3. The alarm was installed by the _____, E. R. Pierce.

4. The company is well known for their _____ quality and service.

5. As I began checking our art collection, I began _____ to myself.

6. I couldn't believe that one of our most prized paintings was gone; it had been the _____ of the collection, my favorite.

7. We were _____ as to how this could have happened; we had no idea at all.

8. Since the phone wasn't working, we ran down the road to the Roberts' house. We knocked loudly, but Paul Roberts was _____ on the phone and couldn't hear us.

9. His wife has always complained that he _____ their phone.

10. Mary took me _____ and saw the tears of anger and frustration in my eyes. The priceless painting was gone, and we couldn't even call the police!

Vocabulary Words

evident
aside
monopolizes
chatting
muttering
superior
clueless
technology
pride
manufacturer

CHAPTER 27
Personal Finance

Predicting

Circle the definition that seems to best fit each vocabulary word. If you have difficulty, return to the reading on page 116, and underline any context clues you find. These clues can help you guess the word's meaning. When you have made your predictions, check your answers against the Word List below. Use the boxes to checkmark those words whose definitions you missed—these are the words you'll want to study closely.

NOTE: You may want to cover the Word List below with a piece of paper so you don't accidentally see the definitions as you do the Predicting exercise.

☐ 1. **circumstances** (panel 1)
   a. types of belts
   b. conditions around something
   c. circuses

☐ 2. **attitude** (panel 1)
   a. way of thinking
   b. way of dressing
   c. way of singing

☐ 3. **acquire** (panel 3)
   a. to sneeze
   b. to get possession of something
   c. to swim

☐ 4. **compound** (panel 3)
   a. to put on a bandage
   b. to increase by adding
   c. to hurt

☐ 5. **bankrupt** (panel 4)
   a. financially ruined and in debt
   b. caught at a robbery
   c. won the lottery

☐ 6. **seminar** (panel 5)
   a. a large building
   b. a type of pasta
   c. a class

☐ 7. **overextend** (panel 5)
   a. to promise or try to do too much
   b. to drive
   c. to help

☐ 8. **sophisticated** (panel 5)
   a. beautiful
   b. boring
   c. complex

☐ 9. **invest** (panel 5)
   a. to use in a way to make a profit
   b. to eat
   c. to get warm

☐ 10. **diversity** (panel 5)
   a. to do long division
   b. to keep
   c. to have variety

Word List

acquire [ə kwīər′] — v. to get possession of something

attitude [at′ ə tood′] — n. a way of thinking or behaving

bankrupt [bangk′ rupt] — adj. financially ruined and in debt

circumstances [sûr′ kəm stan′ səz] — n. the conditions or facts concerning a person, event, or action

compound [kom′ pound] [kəm pound′] — v. to increase by addition

diversify [di vûr′ sə fī′] — v. to add variety

invest [in vest′] — v. to use something such as money in a way that will profit the owner

overextend [ō′ vûr ik stend′] — v. to promise more (money, time, etc.) than you can actually deliver

seminar [sem′ ə när′] — n. a meeting or class for discussion of a particular subject

sophisticated [sə fis′ tə kā′ təd] — adj. experienced in something and having a complex understanding of it

Interactive Exercise

Answer the following questions:

1. Name as many types of *circumstances* as you can other than financial.

   _____

2. What things are you most interested in *acquiring* during your lifetime? (Hint: Qualities may also be acquired!)

   _____

3. Write some adjectives that may be used to describe the noun *attitude*.

   _____

4. What (or whom) would you describe as *sophisticated*?

   _____

5. Name some ways (other than financial) in which you might *overextend* yourself if you aren't careful.

   _____

6. What are some things that you *invest* in (besides stocks and bonds)?

   _____

7. *Bankrupt* means to be in debt and unable to give any more. We've talked about it in terms of money. In what other ways may people be said to be bankrupt?

   _____

8. Name a type of *seminar* that you'd like to attend.

   _____

Self-Test

▶ Fill in the blanks using the words below.

My financial situation is distressing right now because I'm almost _____. I'm in this situation because I spent way more over the past seven months than I make. I'm about to lose everything that I have.

It seems like I never will learn. Even last month I _____ again when I charged $1,200 on my Visa card for an engagement ring for my girlfriend; plus I spend $600 on rent and $500 on my car payment, plus other bills. My _____ about money has changed from enjoying spending to fearing debt. I actually used to think about _____ in stocks for my future, while now I worry only about how I'm ever going to get caught up with my payments.

One of my friends attended a financial planning _____. At this class, they discussed ways of changing your financial _____, such as writing down every penny you spend, and then asking you to evaluate your own spending. They said that most people concentrate on _____ more money, rather than considering how they actually spend the money that they already have. I thought that a seminar like that would be more _____ or complex and would explain some specific situations about investing in stocks and bonds and where to get all the best deals. I thought that my friend would learn things like how interest is _____. I expected him to learn about how to get a variety of different investments—I think that's called _____, but he learned really practical stuff about how to think about the money he already has.

I'd like to take that same seminar, but I can't afford it. I guess I'll just have to depend on my friend to teach me what he learned. Anyway, I'm going to get past this financial crisis and get back to having some fun!

Vocabulary Words

| acquiring | compounded | overextended | attitude | diversifying |
| seminar | bankrupt | investing | sophisticated | circumstances |

CHAPTER 28

Aviation

Private Pilot Lesson #1

Whether you've been interested in **aviation** all your life, or are newly interested, your first flight lesson is a very exciting time! Lesson #1 happens on the ground; it's called the preflight.

The first thing that each pilot must do before every flight is to complete a preflight
5 **inspection** of the aircraft. This is done to **ensure** (make certain) that the airplane is ready to fly.

The **fuselage**, as well as the airfoils (such as the wings) and all control surfaces (such as the **rudder**), must be checked for wrinkles on the skin. These wrinkles would not just be a **cosmetic** problem, but would indicate that the airframe had been
10 overstressed at some point in the past and may have been weakened by it.

The tires must be checked for proper inflation, and the **antennae** of all radios checked for **secure** attachment to the aircraft.

It is best to always begin your "walk around" in the same direction so that you will be sure to work in a **methodical** way. Use the **diagram** below to learn the names of
15 the aircraft's parts and as a simple reminder of what to do.

Have fun with flying, and remember: safety is no accident!

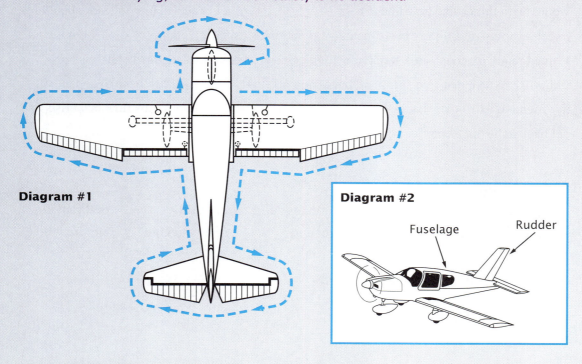

Diagram #1

Diagram #2 — Fuselage, Rudder

Predicting

Circle the definition that seems to best fit each vocabulary word. If you have difficulty, return to the reading on page 120, and underline any context clues you find. These clues can help you guess the word's meaning. When you have made your predictions, check your answers against the Word List below. Use the boxes to checkmark those words whose definitions you missed—these are the words you'll want to study closely.

NOTE: You may want to cover the Word List below with a piece of paper so you don't accidentally see the definitions as you do the Predicting exercise.

☐ 1. **aviation** (line 1)
   a. about birds
   b. about flying and aircraft
   c. about playing cards

☐ 2. **inspection** (line 5)
   a. looking inside one's intentions
   b. looking to the left
   c. a careful examination

☐ 3. **ensure** (line 5)
   a. to be helpful
   b. to be mean
   c. to make certain

☐ 4. **fuselage** (line 7)
   a. a dead body
   b. the body of a plane
   c. anybody

☐ 5. **rudder** (line 8)
   a. a vertical part used for steering
   b. used to stop an illness
   c. red

☐ 6. **cosmetic** (line 9)
   a. the whole universe
   b. appearance and beauty
   c. only on Fridays

☐ 7. **antennae** (line 11)
   a. wires that receive radio signals
   b. homes for ants
   c. a safe place

☐ 8. **secure** (line 12)
   a. beautiful
   b. happy
   c. not likely to fail

☐ 9. **methodical** (line 14)
   a. in a sad way
   b. in a careful, step-by-step way
   c. in a fast way

☐ 10. **diagram** (line 14)
   a. a drawing
   b. a TV show
   c. a movie

Word List

antenna [an ten′ ə]	n.	a wire used to send or receive radio signals (plural : antennae)
aviation [ā′ vē ā′ shən]	n.	having to do with flying, design, or manufacturing aircraft
cosmetic [koz met′ ik]	adj.	concerned with appearance and beauty
diagram [dī′ ə gram]	n.	a drawing showing the parts of something or how it works
ensure [en shûr′] [en shoor′]	v.	to make certain
fuselage [fyoo′ sə läzh′]	n.	the body of an airplane
inspection [in spek′ shən]	n.	a careful examination especially focused on looking for mistakes or trouble
methodical [mə thod′ i kəl]	adj.	done in a careful, step-by-step way
rudder [rud′ ûr]	n.	a vertical part at the rear of a boat or plane that is used for steering
secure [sə kyûr′] [sə kyoor′]	adj.	safe; reliable; not likely to fail

Interactive Exercise

Answer the following questions:

1. Name three places you can find *antennae*. _____

2. Name some jobs connected to *aviation*. _____
   _____

3. Name some concerns or desires that are *cosmetic*. _____
   _____

4. What kinds of *diagrams* have you seen or used? _____
   _____

5. What things do you do every day to *ensure* you health? _____
   _____

6. Describe the shape of a *fuselage*. _____
   _____

7. What *inspections* do you perform on equipment or vehicles you use? _____
   _____

8. Name some jobs that should be done in a *methodical* way. _____
   _____

9. Name some things that have *rudders*. _____
   _____

10. Name some things that you check to make sure that they are *secure*. _____
    _____

Self-Tests

Fill in the blanks using the vocabulary words on page 123.

When I was a little kid, I loved to make paper airplanes. I liked to pretend that I was a pilot and that _____ was my profession.

The paper airplanes that I made flew really well because I was _____ about their construction. I made them with a technique where I folded the vertical piece of paper

CHAPTER 28   AVIATION

that was the _____ so that the airplane turned in the direction I wanted it to when I flew it.

The body (_____) didn't look so good since it was just a flat piece of paper, so I applied paint and got a pretty nice _____ effect with it—it looked good! I even added _____ to my later models, but of course there was no radio actually sending or receiving any signals. They were just toothpicks, cut really short to look right.

After I had finished making the model airplane, I gave it a final _____ to make sure that I'd done everything in my plan. I liked to _____ that everything was complete before the first flight. Once I was certain that all the glue was dry and all antennae were _____, I'd fly the little toy airplane. I must have done a pretty good job because nothing ever fell off.

I used to look at _____ of real airplanes and change my designs to keep up with the industry. I haven't made a paper airplane in years, but it's fun to remember now.

Vocabulary Words
antennae
aviation
cosmetic
diagrams
ensure
fuselage
inspection
methodical
rudder
secure

> **2** Match the vocabulary words below with the correct definition.

_____ 1. I want to make sure.

_____ 2. We need to have one of these, or we won't be able to steer.

_____ 3. Since I was a kid, this has been an interest for me. I even made paper airplanes all the time.

_____ 4. If this fell off the airplane during flight, it might hurt someone on the ground.

_____ 5. This is the manner in which the preflight inspection should always be done.

_____ 6. I used this to make certain that I was doing the inspection correctly.

_____ 7. Inside this is where the passengers sit.

_____ 8. One of these is done before every flight.

_____ 9. It looks beautiful, but I worry if it is as safe as it looks.

_____ 10. I checked to see that all was safe.

Vocabulary Words

| antenna | ensure | methodical | aviation | fuselage |
| rudder | cosmetic | inspection | secure | diagram |

CHAPTER 29

Languages

A Language Vacation

"They say the best way to learn a language is to go to the country where it is spoken. If I go to Spain or Latin America to study Spanish, I can go out and practice with the locals when class is over. That's something I can't do if I take it here on campus. It would be a lot more fun over there, too—combining study and travel. Plus, if I hear everybody around me speaking it, I'll learn a lot faster. That's what they call 'language acquisition,' according to my roommate. He knows all about language because he's majoring in **linguistics**. So anyway, I've been saving up my money and now I have to decide where to go . . . hey, this magazine has some good ads. Here's one for a school in Spain. Hmmm . . . ."

Come and learn Spanish in sunny Spain!

Immerse yourself in a new language and culture for a year, a semester, or a summer.

At **Instituto Quijote** we offer:

— **Intensive** study programs: 5 days, 4 hours daily.
We **tailor** our programs to your individual needs:
Start when you want at the level you require.
— Professional instructors with **ample** experience and advanced degrees
— Weekend **cultural** excursions: Toledo, El Escorial, and other popular sites
— Activity class **options**: dance, cooking, art, music, sports
— **Accommodations**: private homes, dormitories, or hotels
— **Congenial**, friendly atmosphere

For **further** information call 1-800-QUI-JOTE or e-mail: Dferrel@aol.com

Predicting

Circle the definition that seems to best fit each vocabulary word. If you have difficulty, return to the reading on page 124, and underline any context clues you find. These clues can help you guess the word's meaning. When you have made your predictions, check your answers against the Word List below. Use the boxes to checkmark those words whose definitions you missed—these are the words you'll want to study closely.

NOTE: You may want to cover the Word List below with a piece of paper so you don't accidentally see the definitions as you do the Predicting exercise.

❏ 1. **linguistics** (line 8)
   a. scientific study of language
   b. Chinese
   c. foreign studies

❏ 2. **immerse** (line 12)
   a. to stay in the pool
   b. to study
   c. to surround

❏ 3. **intensive** (line 15)
   a. intentional
   b. concentrated
   c. tense

❏ 4. **tailor** (line 16)
   a. to adapt
   b. to claim
   c. to trust

❏ 5. **ample** (line 18)
   a. example
   b. large amount
   c. angle

❏ 6. **cultural** (line 20)
   a. touristy
   b. peaceful
   c. ethnic

❏ 7. **options** (line 22)
   a. choices
   b. exercises
   c. classes

❏ 8. **accommodations** (line 23)
   a. accelerations
   b. organizations
   c. places to stay

❏ 9. **congenial** (line 24)
   a. pleasing
   b. funny
   c. ingenious

❏ 10. **further** (line 25)
   a. ugly
   b. more
   c. heavier

Word List

accommodations [ə kom′ ə dā′ shənz] *n.* rooms; lodging

ample [am′ pəl] *adj.* large in size or amount

congenial [kən jēn′ yəl] *adj.* friendly; pleasant

cultural [kul′ chûr əl] *adj.* relating to the different ways of life of a group of people; ethnic

further [fûr′ THûr] *adj.* more; additional; greater

immerse [i mûrs′] *v.* to surround; to absorb

intensive [in ten′ siv] *adj.* concentrated

linguistics [ling gwis′ tiks] *n.* scientific study of language

option [op′ shən] *n.* choice; alternative

tailor [tā′ lûr] *v.* to adapt

Interactive Exercise

You've decided you're definitely going to Instituto Quijote this summer. Now it's time to fill out your application. In the essay question use at least seven vocabulary words.

Application for Admission
Instituto Quijote

Name: _____

Address: _____

Phone number: _____ Date of arrival: _____

How long will you stay? _____

Accommodations desired: hotel   dormitory   private home

Type of program desired: *intensive*   *semi-intensive*

Class *options* desired: _____

Cultural excursions desired: _____

Your level of Spanish: beginning   intermediate   advanced

Essay question: Why do you want to study Spanish at our language school?

_____
_____
_____
_____
_____
_____

Self-Tests

1 Fill in the blanks with the correct vocabulary words from the list here.

1. _____ can be studied in college.

2. Immigrants to the U.S. come from many _____ backgrounds.

126   CHAPTER 29   LANGUAGES

3. Summer school courses are usually _____; you study a lot of material in a short period of time.

4. You have several _____: take the bus, get a ride from a classmate, or drive your own car to school.

5. Sometimes Peter is so _____ in his reading that I hate to bother him.

6. In some cities it is hard for tourists to find nice _____ at a reasonable price.

7. Please say nothing _____ to us about your idea. We're not interested.

8. There was _____ room in the garage for two cars.

9. The store offered to have the suit _____ to fit him.

10. I had no idea that the staff at the school would be so kind and _____.

Vocabulary Words

accommodations
ample
congenial
cultural
further
immersed
intensive
linguistics
options
tailored

  Circle the correct answers from the choices given in the letter below.

Dear Jake,

How are you? You asked me to tell you a little about my language vacation experience. Well, summer is a great time to travel and learn something new about our world. I decided to go to Mexico last year to study Spanish. I was a beginner, so I picked an (immerse, intensive) program at a university in the central part of the country. This was my first time out of the U.S., and I wanted to have as many new (option, cultural) experiences as possible. The school (tailored, optioned) a course especially for my needs. My (congenial, accommodations) in Mexico were not what I was used to back home. I stayed in a private home with a family because I really wanted to (immerse, further) myself in the language and culture of Mexico. My family was so (ample, congenial) that it would have been easy to just stay home with them. But, there were some great (immerse, options) that I selected, you know—tours, classes, even parties. There was (intensive, ample) opportunity to see the country and get to know the locals.

Jake, if there is anything (ample, further) I can help you with, let me know. Now, I'm back to the books. By the way, I'm taking (options, linguistics) now because I've gotten really interested in language.

Take care and write,
John

CHAPTER 30

Review: Focus on Chapters 22–29

For instructions, see page 129.

1. _____

2. _____

3. _____

4. _____

5. _____

6. _____

7. _____

8. _____

9. _____

10. _____

11. _____

12. _____

13. _____

14. _____

15. _____

The following activities give you a chance to interact some more with the vocabulary words you've been learning. By looking at art, acting, writing, taking tests, and doing a crossword puzzle, you will see which words you know well and which you still need to work with.

Art

Match each picture on page 128 with one of the following vocabulary words. Use each word once.

Vocabulary Words

commercial	sequence	attitude	superlative	antennae
monotonous	downsizing	sophisticated	chat	technology
burden	ample	rudder	fuselage	villainous

Drama

Charades: You will be given one of the following words to act out in class. Think about how this word can be demonstrated without speaking. The other people in class will try to guess what word you are showing.

forecast, retain, generate, blunder, admirable, interrupt, acquiring, overextending, clueless, intensive, panned, inspection, methodical, muttering, resemblance

Writing

Answer the following questions to further test your understanding of the vocabulary words.

1. Do you believe that the U. S. actually has any *superfluous* money available for good causes? Where do you think this money is, and how do you think it should be spent?
   _____
   _____

2. When the word *pride* is mentioned, do you think of it in a positive way, or as something negative? _____

3. Are you concerned about the *security* of your doors and windows at night?
   _____

4. When would you not see a movie or read a book because of what *critics* say?
   _____
   _____

5. For what honors would you like to *qualify* when you graduate from college?
   _____

6. Under what *circumstances* would you accept money from a friend for doing a small favor that cost you nothing? _____
   _____

7. If you won an all-expense-paid trip to Hawaii for the weekend, what would you want the *accommodations* to be like when you arrived? _____
   _____

8. Can you think of a time when *bureaucracy* interfered with your life?
   _____

9. What is the name of the *manufacturer* of your favorite ice cream?
   _____

10. What career *options* are you considering? _____
    _____

11. What sort of news should be *broadcast* more often? _____
    _____

12. What amount of money would you consider *sufficient* so that you would never need to work again? _____

13. What are some of the things that you might do differently if you decided to *diversify* your activities? _____
    _____

14. Some people are opera buffs. Some are hockey buffs. What kind of *buff* are you?
_____

Self-Tests

1 Choose the word that best completes the sentence.

1. I'd like to talk to you alone today. Maybe we can meet after work and have a little _____ over coffee?
    a. antenna   b. chat   c. mutter   d. rudder

2. The yard needs to be mowed. I know that you have a lot of homework, but doing one more chore shouldn't be too much of a _____ for such an energetic person as yourself.
    a. downsize   b. blunder   c. resemblance   d. burden

3. This computer software is very _____; it's too complicated for me.
    a. sophisticated   b. admirable   c. superlative   d. overextended

4. He used four _____ when he praised me: I'm the best secretary he's ever had, I'm the employee with the best attendance record, my attitude is better than anyone else's in the company, and my personality is the most outgoing of anyone in the office.
    a. blunders   b. superlatives   c. resemblances   d. mutterings

5. I noticed that he was asking the store clerk to make change from a twenty-dollar bill, but he told her that he didn't get the correct change from her. We later learned that he was a scam artist who also cheats elderly people out of their Social Security benefits. That man is absolutely _____.
    a. sophisticated   b. intensive   c. villainous   d. admirable

6. I've been _____ skills in the Spanish language. It has happened over a period of time, but I believe that I'm beginning to know how to speak it!
    a. downsizing   b. muttering   c. acquiring   d. overextending

7. The man was very angry after the incident. He walked away _____ something about getting even. It was scary.
    a. blundering   b. downsizing   c. chatting   d. muttering

8. In the TV series *My Favorite Martian,* the only way we knew that one character was a Martian was because he had _____ that grew out of his head when he became excited. He looked like he could pick up radio signals with them.
    a. antennae   b. rudders   c. fuselages   d. tomes

9. When Madonna came to our music class, she _____ a lot of excitement.
    a. blundered   b. generated   c. chatted   d. muttered

10. I was trying to count the change from my piggy bank when my aunt repeated a long-distance telephone number and then an address. Hearing all those other numbers broke the _____ of my counting. I had to start all over again.
    a. burden   b. sequence   c. resemblance   d. superlative

Finish the story using the vocabulary words below. There will be five words left over.

Here is my version of how things happened. I'll give you the events in _____ order because it's easier to understand when you see what happened first, then second, etc. I was sitting at home watching a really interesting _____ about sea birds. I'm an _____ bird-watcher, so I watch a lot of fact-filled programs about birds. Unfortunately, the _____ became so bad that I had to turn the set off. There was no _____ cause for the problem with my TV, so I decided to _____ with the situation in the best way that I could and find something else to do.

I decided to read a book, so I reached for a _____ that was sitting on the bookshelf. It was a mystery—pure _____, of course. The characters were more _____ instead of being interesting individual characters. I was getting bored, so I decided to go to the kitchen, when the doorbell rang.

At the door was my friendly neighbor, Marianne. She wanted to know if I knew anything about why the cable had gone out. I didn't know, but I invited her in for a snack. She's always so easy to get along with and _____ that I was thinking that this might be a better way to spend the evening anyway. She is educated, has an interest in languages, and even has a degree in _____.

We had a snack in the kitchen, then went back into the den to see if the TV was back on. It wasn't working yet, so I put it on the "mute" so that we could talk until it came on again. Unfortunately, she began telling a _____ story about her _____ at her work. I fell asleep!

When I woke up Marianne was asleep next to me, and my wife was standing there staring at us. The TV was on and, much to my _____ horror, Marianne had switched the channel to one with a movie featuring people wearing very few clothes. I took the _____ to explain to my wife what had really happened.

Vocabulary Words
apparent
aside
avid
chronological
compounds
congenial
cope
cultural
documentary
fiction
genuine
initiative
investing
linguistics
monotonous
reception
regimen
stereotypes
supervisor
tome

132 CHAPTER 30 REVIEW

Crossword Puzzle

Use the following words to complete the crossword puzzle. You will use each word once.

Vocabulary Words

adequate
contrived
further
immerse
nightly
bankrupt
cosmetic
fuselage
monopolizing
seminars
category
diagram
host
narrator
superior
contention
dictation
hype
newscast
tailored

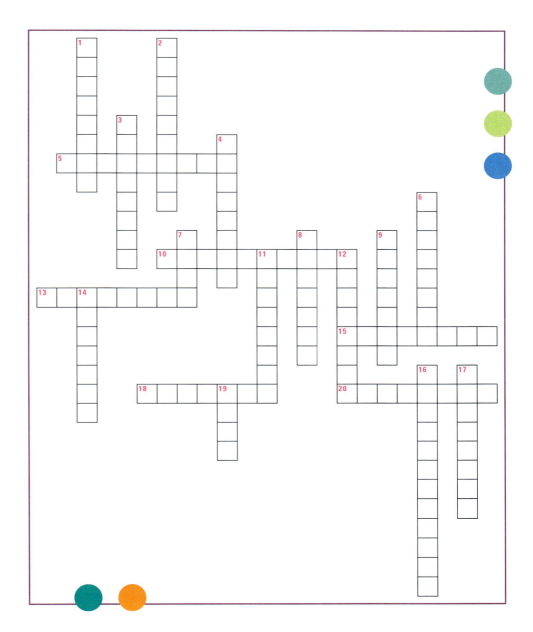

Across
5. set-up
10. I hate it when this happens; sometimes people don't speak.
13. "I've got no money in my account."
15. a type of surgery
18. more
20. clothes altered to fit a particular person

Down
1. We all have one of these at work.
2. a secretarial skill
3. larger than a detail
4. not a comment you'd like to hear about your skills
6. cigar-shaped body
7. the person who welcomes you
8. You might consult one of these in a parts manual for your car.
9. happens in the bathtub, too
11. that voice with no body
12. *World News Tonight with Peter Jennings*
14. the moon and stars
16. very annoying during a conversation
17. You could attend one of these to learn to flirt.
19. There is a lot of this before a movie comes out.

Analogies Appendix

An **analogy** is a comparison. Analogies begin with a pair of words that have a specific relationship with each other. For example:

worry : frown

In an analogy, the colon (:) stands for "is to." When you see the colon, you need to ask yourself, "What is the relationship between those two words?"

QUESTION: What is the relationship between *worry* and *frown?*
ANSWER: *Worry* is an emotion, and a *frown* is the facial expression of that emotion.

The second part of the analogy is a second pair of words that have the same relationship as the words in the first part of the analogy. The double colon (::) means that you need to put together another pair of words that have the same relationship as the first pair of words.

Easy Steps for Doing Analogies

1. Figure out the relationship between the first pair of words.
2. Repeat the same type of relationship in the second pair of words.

Just for practice, match the pairs of words in the left-hand column with the pairs of words in the right-hand column. The answers appear below.

1. car : engine ::
2. entertainment : video games ::
3. pleasure : fun ::
4. sport : work ::
5. worry : frown ::

a. black : white
b. camera : lens
c. book : cookbook
d. pretty : good-looking
e. joy : smile

ANSWERS

1. b [an engine is **part of** a car; a lens is **part of** a camera]
2. c [video games are a **type of** entertainment; a cookbook is a **type of** book]
3. d [**similar** meanings (synonyms); **pleasure** is the same as **fun**, and **pretty** is the same as **good-looking**]
4. a [**opposite** meanings (antonyms); **sport** is the opposite of **work**, and **black** is the opposite of **white**]
5. e [worry is an **emotion**, and a frown is the **facial expression of** that emotion; joy is an **emotion**, and a smile is the **facial expression of** that emotion]

Limited Answer Key

Getting Started
Which Dictionary Should I Buy?
1. f   3. d   5. c   7. e
2. g   4. b   6. a

CHAPTER 1 Cafeteria Views
Predicting
1. c   3. b   5. a   7. b   9. c
2. b   4. a   6. c   8. c   10. a

Self-Test 1
1. c   3. b   5. a   7. i   9. h
2. d   4. e   6. j   8. g   10. f

CHAPTER 2 Sports
Predicting
1. a   3. c   5. a   7. c   9. b
2. b   4. b   6. a   8. b   10. a

Self-Test 1
1. T
2. T
3. T
4. F
5. T
6. T
7. F
8. F
9. T
10. T

CHAPTER 3 School
Predicting
1. c   3. a   5. b   7. a   9. a
2. b   4. c   6. b   8. c   10. c

Self-Test 1
1. e   3. i   5. a   7. h   9. g
2. j   4. f   6. c   8. b   10. d

CHAPTER 4 Music
Predicting
1. c   3. b   5. a   7. c   9. a
2. b   4. c   6. c   8. c   10. a

Self-Test 1
1. soprano
2. rehearsal
3. aptitude
4. experts
5. enchanting
6. chorus
7. novices
8. feedback
9. revue
10. bass

CHAPTER 5 Communication
Predicting
1. a   3. c   5. a   7. c   9. c
2. a   4. b   6. c   8. a   10. b

Self-Test 1
1. philosophical
2. await
3. ponder
4. scroll
5. correspond
6. chisel
7. jot
8. loathe
9. access
10. tome

CHAPTER 6 Word Parts I
Self-Test 1
1. predict
2. relate
3. collaborate
4. manage
5. chronological
6. philosopher
7. enchantment
8. passionate
9. imitation
10. courageous

CHAPTER 7 Romance
Predicting
1. a   3. a   5. a   7. a   9. c
2. a   4. c   6. c   8. c   10. b

Self-Test 1
1. attractive
2. intimidated
3. harmless
4. manipulative
5. impress
6. errand
7. gorgeous
8. established
9. genuine
10. relate

CHAPTER 8 Art
Predicting
1. b   3. c   5. b   7. a   9. c
2. a   4. c   6. a   8. b   10. b

Self-Test 1
1. c   3. d   5. b   7. g   9. j
2. a   4. e   6. h   8. f   10. i

CHAPTER 9 Time Management
Predicting
1. c   3. b   5. b   7. a   9. b
2. a   4. c   6. c   8. b   10. b

Self-Test 1
1. intention
2. accomplish
3. procrastinate
4. productive
5. prioritize
6. efficient
7. frazzled
8. task
9. disorganized
10. management

CHAPTER 10 Review: Focus on Chapters 1–9
Art
1. tome
2. triumph
3. scroll
4. chorus
5. gallery
6. revelation
7. correspond
8. novice
9. gorgeous
10. frazzled
11. opposition
12. campus
13. disorganized
14. stunning
15. chisel

Self-Test 1
1. intimidated
2. pondered
3. deadline
4. grueling
5. interactive
6. apply
7. context clues
8. expert
9. antonyms
10. procrastinated
11. regimen
12. dedicated
13. access
14. feedback
15. task

CHAPTER 11 Personalities
Predicting
1. b   3. c   5. a   7. a   9. c
2. c   4. c   6. b   8. b   10. b

Self-Test 1
1. a   3. d   5. c   7. h   9. g
2. b   4. e   6. j   8. i   10. f

CHAPTER 12 History
Predicting
1. c   3. b   5. a   7. c   9. a
2. a   4. c   6. b   8. c   10. c

Self-Test 1
1. uncharted
2. preliminary
3. remarkable
4. disclosed
5. authenticity
6. hieroglyphics
7. archaeologists
8. accurate
9. chronological
10. manuscript

CHAPTER 13 Politics
Predicting
1. c   3. b   5. b   7. c   9. b
2. a   4. a   6. c   8. b   10. a

Self-Test 1
1. inconvenience
2. queue
3. proxies
4. absentee
5. identity
6. verified
7. proposition
8. polls
9. ballot
10. candidates

CHAPTER 14 Friendship
Predicting
1. b   3. a   5. c   7. a   9. b
2. b   4. c   6. c   8. a   10. a

Self-Test 1
1. gossip
2. give sympathy
3. poor advice
4. malicious gossip
5. give empathy
6. good advice
7. gossip
8. give sympathy
9. keep confidential
10. malicious gossip

CHAPTER 15 Travel
Predicting
1. b   3. c   5. b   7. c   9. c
2. c   4. c   6. a   8. a   10. c

Self-Test 1
1. expenses
2. budgeted
3. excursions
4. souvenirs
5. timetable
6. estimated
4. sightseeing
8. attendant
9. approached
10. reservations

CHAPTER 16 Pets
Predicting
1. b   3. c   5. a   7. c   9. a
2. a   4. b   6. b   8. c   10. c

Self-Test 1
1. clumsy
2. vital
3. noble
4. bereavement
5. affront
6. prognosis
7. invincible
8. unbridled
9. epitaph
10. cope

CHAPTER 17 The Environment
Predicting
1. b   3. c   5. b   7. a   9. b
2. b   4. c   6. a   8. a   10. c

Self-Test 1
1. trend
2. avid
3. benefit
4. global
5. depletion
6. stimulate
7. anticipate
8. endanger
9. cooperate
10. awareness

CHAPTER 18 Word Parts II
Self-Test 1
1. productive
2. nobly
3. inspection
4. generate
5. memorize
6. invincible
7. evident
8. illogical
9. doable
10. manuscript

CHAPTER 19 Volunteering
Predicting
1. b   3. c   5. a   7. b   9. c
2. a   4. c   6. b   8. a   10. a

Self-Test 1
1. elderly
2. commitment
3. empower
4. associated
5. encourage
6. devote
7. realistic
8. appreciation
9. affliction
10. disabled

CHAPTER 20 Complaints
Predicting
1. c   3. c   5. b   7. a   9. c
2. a   4. c   6. b   8. b   10. b

Self-Test 1
1. assume
2. resolve
3. irate
4. clarify
5. overdue
6. threaten
7. claim
8. offensive
9. neglect
10. jeopardize

CHAPTER 21 Review: Focus on Chapters 11–20
Art
1. lament
2. queue
3. threatening
4. excursion
5. ballot
6. disabled
7. nobly
8. souvenir
9. tenderness
10. reservation
11. hieroglyphics
12. gossip
13. epitaph
14. elderly
15. depletion

Self-Test 1
1. appreciation
2. expenses
3. estimate
4. preliminary
5. resolved
6. cope
7. admired
8. encouraged
9. remarkable
10. awareness
11. verify
12. loyal
13. malicious
14. affronted
15. identity
16. invincible
17. benefit
18. empowered
19. assumed
20. apparently

CHAPTER 22 Television
Predicting
1. b   3. c   5. a   7. b   9. c
2. a   4. a   6. a   8. b   10. c

Self-Test 1
1. commercials
2. reception
3. broadcasts
4. newscast
5. nightly
6. forecasts
7. interrupted
8. host
9. documentary
10. narrators

CHAPTER 23 Books
Predicting
1. a   3. b   5. c   7. c   9. c
2. b   4. a   6. b   8. a   10. b

Self-Test 1
1. critics
2. monotonous
3. contention
4. panned
5. superfluous
6. burden
7. resemblance
8. fiction
9. prose
10. stereotypes

CHAPTER 24 Movies
Predicting
1. b   3. b   5. a   7. a   9. c
2. c   4. a   6. a   8. b   10. c

Self-Test 1
1. go on about
2. behave badly
3. make a mistake
4. create
5. fake
6. a logical group
7. has the skill
8. first this, then this
9. excited about
10. greatest

CHAPTER 25 The Workplace
Predicting
1. c   3. b   5. c   7. a   9. b
2. a   4. c   6. b   8. c   10. a

Self-Test 1
a**d**mirable
suff**i**cient
burea**u**cracy
timely
adequate
re**t**ain
initiative
supervis**o**r
dow**n**sizing

CHAPTER 26 Computers

Predicting
1. b 3. b 5. a 7. c 9. b
2. c 4. c 6. a 8. a 10. b

Self-Test 1
1. mutter
2. superior
3. clueless
4. manufacturer
5. monopolize
6. pride
7. chat
8. technology
9. evidently
10. aside

CHAPTER 27 Personal Finance

Predicting
1. b 3. b 5. a 7. a 9. a
2. a 4. b 6. c 8. c 10. c

Self-Test 1
1. bankrupt
2. overextended
3. attitude
4. investing
5. seminar
6. circumstances
7. acquiring
8. sophisticated
9. compounded
10. diversifying

CHAPTER 28 Aviation

Predicting
1. b 3. c 5. a 7. a 9. b
2. c 4. b 6. b 8. c 10. a

Self-Test 1
1. aviation
2. methodical
3. rudder
4. fuselage
5. cosmetic
6. antennae
7. inspection
8. ensure
9. secure
10. diagrams

CHAPTER 29 Languages

Predicting
1. a 3. b 5. b 7. a 9. a
2. c 4. a 6. c 8. c 10. b

Self-Test 1
1. linguistics
2. cultural
3. intensive
4. options
5. immersed
6. accommodations
7. further
8. ample
9. tailored
10. congenial

CHAPTER 30 Review: Focus on Chapters 22–29

Art
1. technology
2. commercial
3. burden
4. fuselage
5. villainous
6. antennae
7. chat
8. superlative
9. attitude
10. sequence
11. downsizing
12. ample
13. rudder
14. monotonous
15. sophisticated

Self-Test 1
1. b 3. a 5. c 7. d 9. b
2. d 4. b 6. c 8. a 10. b

Flash Cards

CHAPTER 1 CAFETERIA VIEWS

analogy
[ə nal′ ə jē]

antonym
[an′ tə nim′]

collaborative
[kə lab′ ûr ə tiv′]

context clues
[kon′ tekst klo͞oz′]

diligent
[dil′ ə jənt]

interactive
[in′ tûr ak′ tiv]

phonics
[fon′ iks]

predict
[pri dikt′]

synonym
[sin′ ə nim′]

thematic
[thē mat′ ik]

n. word that means the opposite	n. a comparison; likeness
n. words around another word that give hints about its meaning	adj. working together
adj. requiring active thought and communication; making connections	adj. steady and energetic; careful
v. to tell in advance	n. a reading method in which letters are associated with their sounds
adj. pertaining to a subject or topic	n. word with a similar meaning

CHAPTER 2 SPORTS

confront [kən frunt']	**dedicated** [ded' ə kā' tid] **dedicate** [ded' ə kāt']
fluke [flo͞ok]	**fluster** [flus' tûr]
grueling [gro͞o' ə ling]	**intense** [in tens']
opposition [äp' ə zish' ən]	**regimen** [rej' ə mən, -men']
stunning [stun' ing]	**triumph** [trī' əmpf]

adj. devoted to a cause v. to give one's talents to; to devote	v. to face head on
n. a state of confusion v. to upset; to cause confused behavior	n. a lucky chance
adj. to an extreme degree; deep	adj. tiring; exhausting
n. a plan; discipline	n. a contestant you are matched against; disagreement
v. to win; to overcome n. the joy of victory	adj. impressive in excellence or beauty; amazing

CHAPTER 3 SCHOOL

apply [ə plī′]	assessment [ə ses′ mənt]
campus [kam′ pəs]	career [kə rēr′]
counselor [koun′ sə lûr]	deadline [ded′ līn]
faculty [fak′ əl tē]	major [mā jûr]
orientation [ôr′ ē ən tā′ shən]	registration [rej′ ə strā′ shən]

n. testing; evaluation	v. 1. to make a formal request 2. (apply oneself) to try hard
n. a profession or occupation	n. buildings and grounds of a school, college, or university
n. latest possible time for something to be completed	n. advisor; person who counsels
n. principal area of study	n. teachers of a school, college, or university
n. formal process of entering a class or program	n. program intended to help people adapt

CHAPTER 4 MUSIC

aptitude
[ap′ tə tōōd′]

bass
[bās]

chorus
[kôr′ əs]

enchanting
[en chan′ ting]

expert
[ek′ spûrt]
[ik spûrt′]

feedback
[fēd′ bak′]

novice
[nov′ is]

rehearsal
[ri hûr′ səl]

revue
[ri vyōō′]

soprano
[sə pran′ ō, -prä′ nō]

n. the singer with the lowest pitch or range	n. 1. talent 2. quickness in learning; intelligence
adj. charming; captivating	n. a group of people singing at the same time v. to sing or speak at the same time
n. a reaction or response to a particular activity	n. a person who has a special skill or knowledge in a field adj. having a special skill from practice
n. a practice, usually for a public performance	n. a beginner
n. the highest singing voice found in some women and in young boys	n. a show featuring skits, songs, and dances

CHAPTER 5 COMMUNICATION

access [ak′ ses]	**await** [ə wāt′]
chisel [chiz′ əl]	**correspond** [kôr′ ə spond′]
jot [jot]	**loathe** [lō TH]
philosophical [fil′ ə sof′ i kəl]	**ponder** [pon′ dər]
scroll [skrōl]	**tome** [tōm]

v. 1. to wait for 2. to be in store for	n. state of being able to approach or enter v. to get
v. 1. to communicate by letter, usually over a period of time 2. to be in agreement	v. to cut or carve n. a metal tool with a sharp edge used to cut stone, wood, or metal
v. to detest; hate	v. to write briefly and fast
v. to consider carefully; reflect	adj. thoughtful; serene; wise
n. any book, especially a large or scholarly book	n. a roll of paper with writing on it

CHAPTER 7 ROMANCE

attractive
[ə trak′ tiv]

errand
[âr′ ənd]

establish
[e stab′ lish]

genuine
[jen′ yoo in]

gorgeous
[gôr′ jəs]

harmless
[härm′ ləs]

impress
[im pres′]

intimidated
[in tim′ i dā təd]

intimidate
[in tim′ i dāt]

manipulative
[mə nip′ yə lə tiv]

manipulate
[mə nip′ yə lāt]

relate
[rē lāt′]

| n.

a thing to do; a routine job | adj.

good-looking |

| adj.

real; true | v.

to form; to make |

| adj.

safe; innocent | adj.

beautiful |

| adj.
scared; frightened

v.
to scare or frighten | v.

to influence |

| v.

1. to connect
2. to tell or report | adj.
using for one's own purposes; controlling

v.
to use for one's own purposes |

CHAPTER 8 ART

abstract [ab strakt′]	**absurdity** [ab sûr′ di tē]
alienation [ā′ lē ə nā′ shən]	**desperation** [des′ pə rā′ shən]
futility [fyoo til′ ə tē]	**gallery** [gal′ ə rē]
obviously [ob′ vē əs lē]	**relevance** [rel′ ə vəns]
revelation [rev′ ə lā′ shən]	**symbolize** [sim′ bə līz′]

| n.

nonsense; foolishness | adj.

disconnected from real life; complex |
|---|---|
| n.

hopelessness; sorrow | n.

division; isolation; distance |
| n.

exhibition room; hall | n.

emptiness; meaninglessness |
| n.

significance; importance | adv.

clearly; plainly |
| v.

to represent; to mean | n.

announcement; discovery |

CHAPTER 9 TIME MANAGEMENT

accomplish [ə käm′ plish]	**disorganized** [dis ôr′ gə nīzd′]
efficient [ē fish′ ənt, i fish′ ənt]	**frazzled** [fraz′ əld]
intention [in ten′ chən]	**management** [man′ ij mənt]
prioritize [prī ôr′ ə tīz′]	**procrastinate** [pro kras′ tə nāt′]
productive [prə duk′ tiv]	**task** [task]

adj. not having order	v. to complete; to carry out
adj. tired; exhausted	adj. orderly; effective
n. direction; control	n. plan
v. to postpone; to put off	v. to place in order of importance
n. assignment; job	adj. able to complete many jobs

CHAPTER 11 PERSONALITIES

admire
[ad mī°r′]

apparent
[ə par′ ənt, ə pâr′-]

fascination
[fas′ ə nā′ shən]

gullibility
[gul′ ə bil′ i tē]

intimate
[in′ tə mit]

lament
[lə ment′]

passionate
[pash′ ən it]

reveal
[ri vēl′]

shrewdness
[shro͞od′ nis]

tenderness
[ten′ dûr nis]

adj. easily seen or understood; clear; evident	v. to think highly of
n. the state of believing too easily and therefore being easily fooled	n. extreme interest; enchantment
v. to express grief	adj. of a very close, personal, or private nature
v. to make known; to display	adj. having strong emotions; enthusiastic; loving
n. warm feelings; softness	n. intelligence; common sense

CHAPTER 12 HISTORY

accurate
[ak′ yûr it]

archaeologist
[är′ kē äl′ ə jist]
archaeology
[är′ kē ol′ ə jē]

authenticity
[ô′ then tis′ ə tē]
authentic
[ô then′ tik]

chronological
[kron′ ə lo′ ji kəl]

disclose
[dis klōz′]

hieroglyphics
[hī′ rō glif′ iks]

manuscript
[man′ yoo skript]

preliminary
[prē lim′ ə nâr′ ē]

remarkable
[rē mär′ kə bəl]

uncharted
[un chär′ təd]

n. one who studies the remains of past human life n. the scientific study of the remains of past human life	adj. correct; exact
adj. arranged in order of time; sequential	n. realness; genuineness adj. real
n. pictorial writing system used in ancient Egypt	v. to make public
adj. beginning; introductory	n. document, generally handwritten
adj. unexplored	adj. great; incredible

CHAPTER 13 POLITICS

absentee [ab′ sən tē′]	**ballot** [bal′ ət]
candidates [kan′ di dāts, kan′ di dits]	**identity** [ī den′ ti tē, i den′ ti tē]
inconvenience [in′ kən vēn′ yəns]	**polls** [pōls]
proposition [prop′ ə zish′ ən]	**proxy** [prok′ sē]
queues [kyōōz]	**verify** [vâr′ ə fī′]

| n.

a form or paper used for voting | n.

a person who is not present |

| n.

a certain person or thing | n.

people who are trying to get elected into office |

| n.

a place where people go to vote | n.

a troublesome occurrence that does not meet one's needs |

| n.

a person who is approved to act for someone who is not present | n.

a plan or offer that is up for approval |

| v.

to say definitely that something is correct | n.

lines of people waiting for something |

CHAPTER 14 FRIENDSHIP

advice [ad vīs′]	**compromise** [kom′ prə mīz]
confidential [kän′ fə den′ chəl]	**empathize** [em′ pə thīz]
gossip [gos′ əp]	**loyal** [loi′ əl]
malicious [mə lish′ əs]	**rift** [rift]
supportive [sə pôr′ tiv]	**sympathy** [sim′ pə thē]

v. to agree by giving up part of what you want	n. an opinion about how to act
v. to identify with another person's situation; to understand his or her feelings	adj. spoken or written for only a few people to know about; secret
adj. not changing in one's devotion to a person, cause, or country	n. 1. information that may be untrue, especially about other people 2. a person who gives information that may be untrue
n. a break or crack	adj. feeling or showing a desire to harm another
n. a feeling of tenderness for another person's pain	adj. giving strength and encouragement

CHAPTER 15 TRAVEL

approach
[ə prōch′]

attendant
[ə ten′ dənt]

budget
[buj′ it]

estimate
[es′ tə māt′]
[es′ tə mit]

excursion
[ik skûr′ zhən]

expenses
[ek spen′ səz]

reservation
[rez′ ûr vā′ shən]

sightseeing
[sīt′ sē′ ing]

souvenir
[sōō′ və nēr′]

timetable
[tīm′ tā′ bəl]

| n.

a person whose duty is to provide a service | v.

to come near |
|---|---|
| v.

to judge the approximate amount of something

n.

a judgment of something's approximate amount | n.

the amount of money or time devoted to a purpose |
| n.

the amount spent in doing something | n.

a short trip |
| n.

visiting places of interest | n.

1. a reserved seat or accommodation
2. reluctance to do something; a doubt |
| n.

1. a list showing arrivals and departures of various types of transportation
2. a schedule showing the times of certain activities | n.

something bought as a reminder of a trip |

CHAPTER 16 PETS

affront
[ə frunt′]

bereavement
[bē rēv′ mənt]

clumsy
[klum′ zē]

cope
[kōp]

epitaph
[ep′ i taf′]

invincible
[in vin′ sə bəl]

nobly
[nō′ blē]
noble
[no′ bəl]

prognosis
[prog no′ sis]

unbridled
[un brīd′ əld]

vital
[vīt′ əl]

n. period of mourning following a death	n. insult v. to insult
v. to survive; to manage	adj. moving with difficulty; awkward
adj. unconquerable; undefeatable	n. brief statement in memory of the dead, usually on a gravestone
n. medical prediction about chances of survival	adv. admirably; in a dignified way adj. admirable
adj. essential; important	adj. free; unrestricted

CHAPTER 17 THE ENVIRONMENT

anticipate [an tis′ ə pāt′]	**avid** [av′ id]
awareness [ə wâr′ nis]	**benefit** [ben′ ə fit]
cooperate [kō äp′ ə rāt]	**depletion** [di plē′ shən]
endangered [en dān′ jûrd] **endanger** [en dān′ jər]	**global** [glō′ bəl]
stimulate [stim′ yə lāt′]	**trend** [trend]

adj. eager; enthusiastic	v. to look forward to; to expect
n. anything that helps well-being; advantage	n. consciousness; knowledge
n. the act of decreasing something; reduction	v. to work together; to agree
adj. involving the entire Earth; international	adj. the possibility of extinction (to no longer be) v. to expose to danger
n. a general direction in which something tends to move; a leaning	v. to excite; to inspire; to cause to do

CHAPTER 19 VOLUNTEERING

affliction
[ə flik′ shən]

appreciation
[ə prē′ shē ā′ shən]

associated
[ə sō′ sē ā təd, ə sō′ shē ā təd]

commitment
[kə mit′ mənt]

devote
[dē vōt′]
devoted
[dē vō′ tid]

disabled
[dis ā′ bəld]

elderly
[el′ dûr lē]

empower
[em pou′ ûr]

encourage
[en kûr′ ij]

realistic
[rē′ ə lis′ tik]

n. feelings of thanks and gratefulness	n. something that causes pain or distress
n. a duty or promise to do something	adj. to have a connection or relationship with
adj. without certain abilities	v. to dedicate oneself to something; to promise adj. dedicated
v. to give power to	n. old people
adj. based on facts	v. to give hope and confidence to someone

CHAPTER 20 COMPLAINTS

assume [ə so͞om′]	**claim** [klām]
clarify [klâr′ ə fī]	**irate** [ī rāt′]
jeopardize [jep′ ûr dīz]	**neglect** [ni glekt′]
offensive [ô fen′ siv, ə fen′ siv]	**overdue** [ō′ vûr do͞o′]
resolve [rē zôlv′]	**threaten** [thret′ ən]

n. request v. to declare to be true	v. to suppose, to believe
adj. very angry; furious	v. to make clear; to explain
v. to fail to pay attention to; to overlook	v. to risk
adj. past due; tardy	adj. insulting
v. to put in danger	v. to find a solution to; to solve

CHAPTER 22 TELEVISION

broadcast
[brôd′ kast′]

commercial
[kə mûr′ shəl]

documentary
[dok′ yoo men′ tə rē]

forecast
[fôr′ kast′]

host
[hōst]

interrupt
[in′ tə rupt′]

narrator
[nâr′ āt ûr]

newscast
[nooz′ kast′]

nightly
[nīt′ lē]

reception
[rē sep′ shən]

| n.

broadcast advertisement | n.

a program sent out over radio or TV

v.

1. the act of sending out a signal (electronic)

2. to make generally known |
|---|---|
| n.

statement that predicts something

v.

the act of telling in advance what is going to happen | n.

factual dramatized report |
| v.

to break the continuity or flow of something | n.

person who receives another as his or her guest

v.

to act as a host |
| n.

a broadcast news report | n.

the person who tells a story |
| n.

the receiving of electronic signals | adv.

happening every night |

CHAPTER 23 BOOKS

burden
[bûrd′ ən]

contention
[kən ten′ shən]

critic
[krit′ ik]

fiction
[fik′ shən]

monotonous
[mə not′ ən əs]

panned
[pand]

prose
[prōz]

resemblance
[rē zem′ bləns]

stereotype
[stâr′ ē ō tīp′]

superfluous
[soo pûr′ floo əs]

n. an argument	n. a difficult job, task, or load to carry
n. a made-up or invented story; not factual	n. a person whose job is to share his or her opinions, good or bad, about books, movies, art, music, etc.
v. badly criticized	adj. having no variety; boring
n. similarity to another person, place, or thing	n. language that is not poetry
adj. more than is needed	n. a standardized idea or character with no individual features; a set of characteristics used to classify people

CHAPTER 24 MOVIES

blunder
[blun′ dûr]

buff
[buf]

category
[kat′ ə gôr′ ē]

contrived
[kən trīvd′]

generate
[jen′ ə rāt′]

hype
[hīp]

qualify
[kwäl′ ə fī′]

sequence
[sē′ kwəns]

superlative
[soo pûr′ lə tiv]

villainous
[vil′ ə nəs]

n. admirer; follower	n. a mistake v. to make a mistake
adj. lacking spontaneity; artificial; fake	n. a class, group, or division
n. excess promotion	v. to start up; to develop
n. arrangement in a logical order	v. to meet the requirements
adv. evil; very wicked	n. an exaggerated expression, usually of praise

CHAPTER 25 THE WORKPLACE

adequate [ad′ ə kwət]	**admirable** [ad′ mûr ə bəl]
bureaucracy [byoo rok′ rə sē]	**dictation** [dik tā′ shən]
downsizing [doun′ sīz ing]	**initiative** [i nish′ ə tiv]
retain [rē tān′]	**sufficient** [sə fish′ ənt]
supervisor [soo′ pûr vī′ zûr]	**timely** [tīm′ lē]

adj. excellent; worthy of praise or admiration	adj. all right, but not wonderful; satisfactory
n. language that is written down at the same time that it is heard by the writer	n. officially required routine that is overdone; organizational structure that is large and often inefficient
n. the first step toward beginning something	v. making a company smaller by changing jobs around and letting some employees go
adj. enough	v. to keep
adj. happening at the perfect time	n. a person whose job is to be in charge of workers and their work

CHAPTER 26 COMPUTERS

aside
[ə sīd′]

chat
[chat]

clueless
[kloo′ləs]

evidently
[ev′ ə dənt lē, ev′ ə dent′ lē]

evident
[ev′ ə dənt]

manufacturer
[man′ yə fak′ chûr ûr]

manufacture
[man′ yoo fak′ chûr]

monopolize
[mə nop′ ə līz]

mutter
[mut′ ûr]

pride
[prīd]

superior
[sə pēr′ ē ûr]

technology
[tek nol′ ə jē]

v. to have a conversation n. a conversation	adv. 1. away 2. to one side
adv. clearly adj. clear; plain	adj. without understanding; confused
v. to control; to dominate	n. producer; maker v. to produce
n. self-respect; confidence	v. to speak softly and unclearly
n. applied science; system design	adj. 1. showing a feeling of being better than others 2. excellent

CHAPTER 27 PERSONAL FINANCE

acquire [ə kwī⁾r′]	**attitude** [at′ ə tōōd]
bankrupt [bangk′ rupt]	**circumstances** [sûr′ kəm stan′ səz]
compound [kom′ pound, kəm pound′]	**diversify** [di vûr′ sə fī′]
invest [in vest′]	**overextend** [ō′ vûr ik stend′]
seminar [sem′ ə när′]	**sophisticated** [sə fis′ tə kā′ təd]

n.	v.
a way of thinking or behaving	to get possession of something

n.	adj.
the conditions or facts concerning a person, event, or action	financially ruined and in debt

v.	v.
to add variety	to increase by adding

v.	v.
to promise more (money, time, etc.) than you can actually deliver	to use something such as money in a way that will profit the owner

adj.	n.
experienced in something and having a complex understanding of it	a meeting or class for discussion of a particular subject

CHAPTER 28 AVIATION

antenna
[an ten′ ə]

aviation
[ā vē ā′ shən]

cosmetic
[koz met′ ik]

diagram
[dī′ ə gram]

ensure
[en shûr′, en shoor′]

fuselage
[fyoo′ sə läzh′]

inspection
[in spek′ shən]

methodical
[mə thod′ i kəl]

rudder
[rud′ ûr]

secure
[sə kyûr′, sə kyoor′]

n. having to do with flying, design, or manufacturing aircraft	n. a wire used to send or receive radio signals (plural : antennae)
n. a drawing showing the parts of something or how it works	adj. concerned with appearance and beauty
n. the body of an airplane	v. to make certain
adj. done in a careful, step-by-step way	n. a careful examination especially focused on looking for mistakes or trouble
adj. safe; reliable; not likely to fail	n. a vertical part at the rear of a boat or plane that is used for steering

CHAPTER 29 LANGUAGES

accommodations
[ə kom′ ə dā′ shənz]

ample
[am′ pəl]

congenial
[kən jen′ yəl]

cultural
[kul′ chûr əl]

further
[fûr′ THûr]

immerse
[i mûrs′]

intensive
[in ten′ siv]

linguistics
[ling gwis′ tiks]

option
[op′ shən]

tailor
[tā′ lûr]

| adj.

large in size or amount | n.

rooms; lodging |
|---|---|
| adj.

relating to the different ways of life of a group of people; ethnic | adj.

friendly; pleasant |
| v.

to surround; to absorb | adj.

more; additional; greater |
| n.

scientific study of language | adj.

concentrated |
| v.

to adapt | n.

choice; alternative |

Word List

A
absentee, 59
abstract, 37
absurdity, 37
access, 25
accommodations, 125
accomplish, 41
accurate, 55
acquire, 117
adequate, 109
admirable, 109
admire, 51
advice, 63
affliction, 83
affront, 71
alienation, 37
ample, 125
analogy, 9
antenna, 121
anticipate, 75
antonym, 9
apparent, 51
apply, 17
appreciation, 83
approach, 67
aptitude, 21
archaeologist, 55
aside, 113
assessment, 17
associated, 83
assume, 87
attendant, 67
attitude, 117
attractive, 33
authenticity, 55
aviation, 121
avid, 75
await, 25
awareness, 75

B
ballot, 59
bankrupt, 117
bass, 21
benefit, 75
bereavement, 71
blunder, 105
broadcast, 97
budget, 67

buff, 105
burden, 101
bureaucracy, 109

C
campus, 17
candidates, 59
career, 17
category, 105
chat, 113
chisel, 25
chorus, 21
chronological, 55
circumstances, 117
claim, 87
clarify, 87
clueless, 113
clumsy, 71
collaborative, 9
commercial, 97
commitment, 83
compound, 117
compromise, 63
confidential, 63
confront, 13
congenial, 125
contention, 101
context clues, 9
contrived, 105
cooperate, 75
cope, 71
correspond, 25
cosmetic, 121
counselor, 17
critic, 101
cultural, 125

D
deadline, 17
dedicated, 13
depletion, 75
desperation, 37
devote, 83
diagram, 121
dictation, 109
diligent, 9
disabled, 83
disclose, 55
disorganized, 41

diversify, 117
documentary, 97
downsizing, 109

E
efficient, 41
elderly, 83
empathize, 63
empower, 83
enchanting, 21
encourage, 83
endangered, 75
ensure, 121
epitaph, 71
errand, 33
establish, 33
estimate, 67
evidently, 113
excursion, 67
expenses, 67
expert, 21

F
faculty, 17
fascination, 51
feedback, 21
fiction, 101
fluke, 13
fluster, 13
forecast, 97
frazzled, 41
further, 125
fuselage, 121
futility, 37

G
gallery, 37
generate, 105
genuine, 33
global, 75
gorgeous, 33
gossip, 63
grueling, 13
gullibility, 51

H
harmless, 33
hieroglyphics, 55